I Like Alf

For Penny and Elliot

I Like Alf

14 Lessons from the life of Alf Engers

Paul Jones

I Like Alf

14 Lessons from the life of Alf Engers

Copyright © Paul Jones 2018

First published in 2018 by
Mousehold Press
6, Constitution Opening
Norwich, NR3 4BD

www.mousehold-press.co.uk

Cover design by studioade.com

ISBN 978-1-874739-81-4

Printed by Page Bros, Norwich

Contents

Author's Acknowledgements:
Writing a book is hard. Thank you to Adrian Bell for making it less hard, for agreeing with the idea and guiding it through. Without his support and willingness to take risks with unproven writers there would be no manuscript. Adrian Ridley is also a key part of the process. His cover design, enthusiasm and ideas are integral to ensuring that the book looks like I want it to look. Steve Green did some early reads and also agreed to me writing about something that is far more intense and personal for him than it is for me, and for that along with many other things I will always be grateful. Crucially, without Allen Janes this book would be much thinner and poorly researched. He is the default archivist with an endless array of memorabilia and Cycling magazines. We take our cues from North London: the Bristol South Mafia is strong.

I am indebted to the words of lots of incredible writers who were there at the time and wrote peerless accounts of races and people, mostly within the pages of *Cycling*. These include, but are by no means limited to, Alan Gayfer, Ken Evans, Keith Bingham, Bernard Thompson, Sid Saltmarsh, Jock Wadley, Dennis Donovan and David Taylor.

In more recent years, thanks to Jack Thurston – for constructive criticism over a beer at Roll for the Soul, Max Leonard for writing great books and being open to conversation, Chris Sidwells for saying nice things and being encouraging, and Feargal Mackay at podium cafe for his advice and interest. Thank you to Keith Williams for helping me untangle some of the John Woodburn timeline, and also to Peter Whitfield who is always supportive and generous. Ray Pascoe continues in his unheralded role as chief film archivist and I drew on his film about Alf for additional texture and colour.

Thank you to everyone who expressed an interest and enthusiasm for this project, from contemporaries like Dave Le Grys and Mick Ballard, to lifelong fans and people who simply love cycling. This extends to Chris Dyke who took the time to tell me how much he liked the Hill Climb book and why; I felt at that point that it was worth writing. Thank you to Holly Carter and Martin Wilson at Rare Mags, Tim Wilkey at Forever Pedalling, Mike Pope at Strada, and Michael and

Helen Broadwith. They are all people who try to live life intensely, to do things that make some sort of sense and are true and real.

I owe thanks to Sheila Hardy at the CTT. She is much more than a supporter, she is a friend, a warm and open person who loves cycling and embodies the amateur spirit. There are others, Phil Hurt and Richard Haigh, Dave Braidley, Rob Hutchinson, Bridget and Ian Boon. They expend time and energy to ensure the sport we know and love – in all its idiosyncrasies and contradictions – continues to grow and thrive. This book is a narrative of social change, conflict and tension, but in case I haven't made it clear, I am in awe of the CTT and the work it does, year on year.

Lastly, thank you to my Mum for being amazing; to Mike for his eye for detail; and to Helen, for being fantastic and endlessly supportive in the purest and most profound way.

See you up the road.

Picture Credits:

John Coulson (18); Alf Engers (1, 2, 7, 9, 10, 12, 19, 20, 26, 30);
Judith Engers (34); Larry Hickmott/Velo UK (32); Elliott Jones (24);
Penny Jones (31); North Mymms History Project (p.40);
John Pick (33); Ken Plowman (p.100); David Pountney (21, 22, 25);
Bernard Thompson (11, 13, 14, 15, 17, 18, 23, 27, 28, 29);
Adrian Thornton (16,16a); Len Thorpe (3, 5, 6, 8); Unknown (4)

BRISTOW strip cartoon. ©2018.The Estate of Frank Dickens. Dist. Knight Features

...there is no road that is right entirely.

(Louis MacNeice)

The Pedal Club

I am giving a talk at the Pedal Club, an old boys' network for previous professionals and those involved in the industry. It is a roll call of metropolitan cycling and assorted heroes: Grant Young of Condor Cycles; Carlton Kirby; Chalky White from Herne Hill; 6-Day legend Maurice Burton; scientific über-coach Peter Keen; professional roadman Doug Collins. I make a joke to break the ice and calm my nerves: something about how being able to control a thousand teenagers in an assembly makes this a piece of cake. I used the same joke for a different audience and they chuckled; here it meets with riotous laughter, much more than I expected, and I realise it's because they think I'm comparing them to a marauding pack of slightly ill-behaved teenagers, which I wasn't, but it seems to work in my favour.

I get nervous, then more nervous, then realise it's ok because that's probably what they actually are: chaps having fun with added wine and reliving their youth and talking about the thing they love, in the way that teenagers are able to do, unencumbered by the world around them. I think I get away with it. I can see Steve Green, a fellow writer and filmmaker from Bristol, who has come along for moral support, having been through this cauldron some months previously, telling Tour of Britain veterans what it means to be a Tour of Britain veteran and showing them footage of their younger selves. At times like this it is easy to be overwhelmed by imposter syndrome. I muddle through, showing them pictures of themselves and talking about them. At the end, I wait for the customary Q&A.

Maurice Burton rises from his seat. I'm excited and nervous; I have seen him in pictures, circling the Ghent track with Patrick Sercu, Gary Wiggins, Paul Medhurst, Ian Hallam, Leo Van Vliet, Gerrie Knetemann, Nigel Dean. He's very kind and asks me how I got into cycling, what made me ride and write. I'm stupidly flattered: Maurice Burton is asking me how I got into riding bikes, as though he really cares, and I think he actually does. We talk about Condor Cycles in the company of Grant Young, son of Monty, founder of Condor Cycles, and I begin to wonder if I'm ever going to get over the day's experiences, let alone sitting between Chalky White and Carlton Kirby, talking about Hugh Porter, listening to Doug Collins, who rode for Condor Mackeson, talk about riding a Moulton on David Duffield's instruction, from London to Holyhead, when somewhere along the line it collapsed beneath him.

And there is room for one last question. From the back of the room, to the left, a tall figure rises, wearing worsted, immaculately dressed. Not just that, but individually and sartorially perfect in the way that some people just are. A dandy, a tweed and worsted suit with a pair of cracking brogues, bi-colour, practically solatios crossed with brothel creepers, but worn to perfection. And a twill shirt, checked; neatly cropped hair. A voice starts; it's high pitched, almost abrasive, a nasal, slightly reedy but clear tone, a cockney accent. And I suddenly realise with a jolt that I am about to be asked a question by Alf Engers or, as he is more commonly known in time trial circles, *The King*.

I listen to his question, insofar as I hear some words coming out and pick out something about cycling, I think linked to something I said about Darryl Webster, who appeared in the visual presentation, a super image taken by Paul Wright which formed the cover of my previous book. And it's clear that Alf Engers is a big fan of Darryl Webster, and that he doesn't really ask questions, he makes gnomic statements that don't brook much response. And my response is simple: "I'm slightly addled by the fact that I've just been asked a question by Alf Engers. I will try to answer but, as a committed tester, it's worth bearing in mind that this is a formative moment for me." We discuss, back and forth, how absurdly talented and fast we both think Darryl Webster was. We skirt lightly around the fact that he's a very lively character with some lively views. We end, I think, on similar ground. I summarise by using a line to describe everyone I know who is true to themselves, regardless of what forces or things seem to be lined up against them. I refer to Eddie Carbone from *A View from the Bridge*, or at least, to Alfieri's description of him: 'He allowed himself to be wholly known and for that I will love him more than all my sensible clients.' And we reach an acceptance that we are on the same page. Webster took on the forces at large and won some of the time, but also lost a lot of the time. I make a silent note to try and speak to Alf after we finish, but within moments he has vanished, seemingly never there, and Steve and I have to hotfoot it back to Paddington Station lest we miss our train and have to pay an additional million pounds to the Great Western Railway for the privilege of leaving half an hour later. We escape, emboldened by our experiences and keen to write more words and make more films.

Six weeks later I'm at work and the phone rings. It is an unusual number and unrecognisable area code. I pick up, expecting a PPI call: a silence then an invitation to claim money. There is a silence, but then a voice cuts through. "Hello Paul. Or should I say: 'FIVE... FOUR... THREE... TWO... ONE... GO!'." A tester's call to arms, the push, an acceleration, a quickening of the pulse. All of these things happen. I can't work it out, then suddenly I realise again, with another jolt, I'm talking to ALF ENGERS. No wait... ALF ENGERS HAS RUNG ME.

And the process begins, much as it carries on, with an anecdote. Alf Engers likes an anecdote. He has lots of them, endless vignettes spooling out like the unrolling reels of a C90 cassette, a magnetic record of a lifetime spent cycling and living in London. He rolls through a string of stories like a demented after-dinner speaker, each one shot through with dark, slapstick humour and emblematic of some aspect of British cycling: the outdoor tracks; the indoor Skol track; the men in blazers; road-racing; the Finsbury Park circuit; the blazers; rules and regulations; early starts; the blazers; match fishing for huge carp; training with the Barnet CC; more about the blazers. Names roll off the tongue: Ray Booty, Beryl Burton, Tommy Simpson, Eileen Sheridan, Ian Hallam, John Woodburn, Peter Post, Gordon Ian – each one a legend, with encounters and battles won and lost. I scrawl as much as I can in a notebook and we make plans to meet; he wants me to write it all down. I say yes before I can say no.

I listen to his anecdotes, and I listen intently to the silences, the pauses, an aphasia caused by waves of feeling and people emerging from the depths of time, both living and dead. A memory is hinted at, underscored, a silence roars into life, a change in tone driven by a tinder-dry memory which suddenly catches into flame: "You shouldn't have said that, you really shouldn't have, Paul." In the photos he is young, sprightly, far younger than me, now in this room. The memories are reified with emotional heft, weighing down each word, and making past realities and experiences once again real and tangible, such is the vivid power of reminiscence and of talk.

As I talk to Alf, or listen, I'm aware of different eras, different times, and different people. There is the person to whom I'm talking now, in the room, rolling through the archive. Then, there is who he was in that moment, when the events unfolded. And somehow there is a liminal person, mediating all of this, all of the events, the interviews conducted and thoughts expressed; reviewing it, reflecting on it, wanting to make sense of it. This book is a record of unravelled feelings and thoughts, failings and successes. It is about Alf Engers, but concurrently about something in all of us, a shared thread of feelings which transcend our physical limitations, it is about 'the tremor of eternity'[1], a thread which spools through time and includes us all, which at a certain age, begins to 'flash and horrify' and urges us to make sense of things somehow.

It stands plain as a wardrobe, what we know,
Have always known, know that we can't escape.[2]

We meet at his house in Hertfordshire, further north than his old stomping ground. I take him biscuits, of course. He lives with his wife, Judith, and a pack of large black dogs, barking from behind the kitchen door in contained and breathless anger, the hot and wet rasp of dog, and percussive pad of claw on lino. They are disembodied voices, desperate to make me aware that should I enter the kitchen there will be an encounter and it will not end well. Judith reassures me that it's ok and she speaks in a gentle antipodean lilt: "the dogs are waiting to rip your head off." I think she's joking. But, then again, I was late and left Alf Engers, the man for whom time meant more than anything else, waiting at the station far longer than is appropriate.

Our encounters become punctuated by humour and references. Even in the car he gets started on a rolling wave of anecdotes: "We were off to Bournemouth. It was me, John Harvey and John Woodburn. It ended up being a pretty disastrous meeting, and it started badly. We got John Harvey to book the accommodation for the team somewhere. He rang this number and it rang and rang and rang and eventually this bloke answered and went 'Ello' in a really gruff, pained way, like he was really cross. John told him he wanted to book accommodation for however many people and the bloke said, 'Right I'll put it in the book,' and slammed the phone down.

"We got to this address later in the week and this chap took ages to get to the door. We could hear him thumping around and wondered what the hell was going on. Eventually he opened the door and he's balanced on wooden crutches, got his leg in plaster. John Harvey says, 'Hello, I'm John Harvey... er... I rang to book the accommodation?' and he said: 'Yeah... You're the BASTARD who rang when I fell down the bloody stairs'."

And the tone is set.

Lesson 1

Empty vessels make the most noise

Copenhagen Street runs from the King's Cross goods depot in York Way, to the edge of Islington at an angle, like a dog's leg cocked insouciantly against Barnard Park. It owes its Scandinavian name to the Danish ambassador's residence in the seventeenth century, but was previously known as Maiden Lane, nestling gently amidst the green spaces of Copenhagen Fields, the site of London's historic animal markets before the trade shifted to Smithfield. At the turn of the eighteenth century the open space became a crucible of discontent, the venue for radical uprisings and demonstrations against the hierarchy and vested interest. In the era following the French Revolution protests and popular meetings attracted crowds in excess of 100,000. As late as 1834, the fields hosted a huge march in support of the Tolpuddle Martyrs, the anti-establishment and nascent trade unionists from Dorset. Whatever was in the water, besides cholera, it is clear that an anti-establishment zeal ran through the area in rivulets of rebellion.

As such, it seems appropriate that it is the birthplace of Alf Engers. He was born a mile down the Euston Road in University College Hospital on 1 June 1940. Then a formal red-brick building, now a shimmering white, multi-storey PFI build, it is indistinguishable from the gleaming glass and steel tower blocks lining the arterial road. Alf spent his first four years at Copenhagen Street, living through the highest point of the Blitz in 1940 with both daylight and nocturnal attacks a regular occurrence. However, Copenhagen Street wasn't the first location of choice for the Engers family. "My grandparents initially opened a place in Roman Road; it was razed to the ground during the First World War. My mother said it was on account of the German sounding surname that they came in for a lot of flak. Grandfather saw somebody throwing a dustbin through the window and they had to go. They escaped over the rooftops, with his mother clinging to his back and a five shilling bag of copper pennies. That was the end of the first Engers' bakery in the East End."

Alf pronounces 'war' as 'woo-ah', with a heavily London second syllable, utterly London, but also unmistakably Alf. They moved to Copenhagen Street – not the current Copenhagen Street that links the shiny redeveloped concourse of King's Cross with the wealthy squares and splendour of Islington – but a previous incarnation in the 1920s as a light commercial and residential road between a goods yard and a tenement, in the heart of an industrial and commercial city sprawl. They settled in for the long haul, with Alf Engers senior and his mother working hard to establish their Viennese-style bakery, but again up against external forces with different ideas, a post-war volatility and anti-German sentiment embodied by attacks against foreign-sounding businesses and a cagey, war-driven xenophobia.

Copenhagen Street, like so much of London, is a palimpsest, having been built over and built over again, with layers of social history concealed just below the tarmacked city streets, glimpses of it lurking in dated facades and erratic remnants of the past. Now it's all post-war housing and commerce, red-brick, Peabody-style buildings, low-rise tenements of the sort that rose out of the bombsites in the 1950s. Naish Court and York Way Court were completed in the late 1940s, filling the gaps left behind by the *Luftwaffe*. The Church of the Blessed Sacrament lingers on, a foothold against change, a different tone of brick, and a few paler buildings with cream-coloured bits on the top, typical of Islington. It crosses the Caledonian Road, or 'Caley Road', a clogged vein running alongside the furred aorta of the Holloway Road. It is the heart of North London, the hinterland between King's Cross and Archway, a tattered ribbon of houses and shops. The identity of the area has changed many times in the past sixty years. The Mitre, a Charringtons pub, was rebuilt in 1937 and lasted through until sudden changes in zoning and building regulations in 2015 led to a conversion to residential use. The Earl of Warwick survived the war, only to be demolished in 2009, the same fate befell the George IV and the Golden Lion. The latter is now a shiny residential development, three- and four-bedroom houses for those who can afford them.

Alf's father was also an Alf; they are both Alfreds. His grandfather was an Adolf; born in Shepherd's Bush from a German emigré, coming across from Saxe-Coburg, now part of modern Bavaria, and bringing the patisserie secrets with him, even if the name, unsurprisingly, disappeared for good after the Second World War. Alf is reticent about his father. He changes his tone, shifts and quietens. I ask him if he got on with his dad. He answers a different question to the one asked.

He answers with a long pause and audible filler, a super long and nasal "errrr..."

"He was very keen on fishing. Didn't have any time for me. Worked my mother to death. *That's it.*"

And that is pretty much it. I push him on it a few times; he prevaricates. We come back to it. I'm convinced there is something there, a big motivating factor, a silent impulse, a driving force, and there probably is but Alf isn't going anywhere near it. Not yet. Years of repressed memory and emotion have made the inner layers of Alf akin to the layers of time on the London streets. I need a gap, a way of getting beneath and finding the emotional archaeology. I'm looking for aporia, I get details instead.

"He had a first wife who died, I can't remember what of; she was forty-odd. There was a brother and sister who are both dead. There is a family grave in the city of London, grandfather, father, mother, and there was a child, another Alfred, who died of meningitis aged 11 or 12 years old. Dad fought in the First World War, and he was always... well, he told the story of how he did this camp kitchen, which was basically a sheet of tin, you put anything combustible underneath and it had holes cut for saucepans. It was like a baker's oven. He always said he was going to get the VC for that. I think that was upping it. A lot.

"There was nothing I admired about him, however he did suffer from various illnesses. Any guidance in my life was non-existent. I remember asking for a pair of running spikes when I represented the school and he refused, saying it was "just another five minute wonder" – something I've always remembered. I subsequently bought a second-hand pair from someone, and took them home, just to show them I had some. My mother was very hard-working and brought up in the Depression. In other words, she knew what poverty was. Being involved in the bakery was a step up for her. She took the view that there would always be something to eat. Mother helped me in any way she could; she had a will of iron."

Alf senior put his effort into the family bakery, ensuring his wife also put her effort into it, morning noon and night. It's an unforgiving job: savage early mornings that become long, long days and late nights with no pause for breath, and hollow sleep snatched in stuttering seconds between shifts. It consists of manual labour and tough conditions, with Engers senior working the family hard to put bread on the table, literally and metaphorically.

"The bakers would start at 8pm and by midnight the first batch was coming out of the oven. I remember the bread, a lingering smell that gave a baker satisfaction having produced an honest product and something to be proud of. There was a baker's shop on every corner, usually with a loft above. Flour deliveries entailed a ladder with a plank coming across from the lorry. It was a perilous job for the millers if it happened to be raining with a 140lb* bag on their shoulders."

Within four years of Alf's birth in 1940 the second family bakery, like the first, was destroyed. The station and goods yard at King's Cross was a valuable target for the *Luftwaffe*, initially in the blitz from 1940 to 1941, but then following with V1 and V2 rockets.

"Every night there would be air raids and by morning several houses in our area would have been destroyed. I wondered when our time would come. One night the usual air-raid siren went off and people ran for cover to the tube stations. Being a working bakery, we stayed put. V1s used to come over and when they ran out of fuel the noise stopped. We had taken cover in the Morrison shelter, which was not much more than a steel table. It stopped; my mother said, 'It's overhead,' and then there was an almighty thump. I looked out from under the table and the ceiling started to come down and a light bulb over the fridge danced up and down. Everything went quiet, with choking dust. My father said we'd be alright as long as it didn't catch fire. My mother reacted, 'Don't say that!' and threw a quilt over me. The force of the impact had thrown her into the iron post of the table and she was badly hurt. Slowly my father moved the rubble away from one side of the table. By the light of a candle I could see he was covered in a fine white dust."

---

* The publisher asked me to check that weight. Alf confirmed it: "Yeah, it's a bloody big bag. Pre-war they were twice that. I couldn't lift it now."

The premises and nearby houses had been reduced to a seething mass of splintered wood, wattle, batten, bricks, mortar, and strangely still-standing walls with fireplaces and pictures, and curtains fluttering unhurriedly in the breeze. A line of people and ARP teams dug them out, one by one, through the debris and dust. "It felt like hours later when a speck of light appeared and we could hear shouting. I was taken out first, and I looked around: the whole block had been flattened." Underneath the triangular apex of roof beams buried in the earth everything had collapsed in on itself, with the houses around wounded and damaged. The family survived with minor injuries but, tragically, the three night bakers working downstairs were killed.

"I later heard of a retired fireman who recalled the direct hit, and the work to dig us out alive. At the time, father had a room out at Barnet, on Summerswood Farm. We went and lived there." But even the comparable calm of Barnet, out in the Hertfordshire countryside, wasn't beyond the reach of the war.

"You heard these sirens go off and would see the searchlights going in the sky. One night a bomb dropped, it sounded like it was ten yards away, but was about half a mile away, and left a 30-foot crater. There's probably a block of flats there now; it's on a ridge at South Mimms. I liked it there. I would go out looking for vipers, snakes, running and riding round the farm on a little bike. At one point not long after moving we went back to Copenhagen Street; I saw a crane taking the safe out of the ruins, and saw our old Ford Poplar car. You couldn't buy cars during the war; you put your name down and six months later you might have had the opportunity. There was nothing left of the bakery. Since then the ground has been built on at least three times and is now a block of flats. It's not the same street."

After the war the family moved back to London, taking up residence in Elthorne Road in Archway with Engers senior opening the new premises. As he grew up, his relationship with his father failed to improve. "He just wasn't interested. He went fishing and I followed him. He was a match angler. I was a lot more extreme in everything, always. I'd bugger off on my own. I can remember him fishing on the Thames, sitting there, and I sort of swam slowly past his float. I had this habit of getting up people's noses, especially dad's."

Rationing was still very much in force, and would continue to be for some time. "When you went to a grocer's you had King Edward potatoes, beetroot, Webb's lettuce; things like mushrooms were non-existent. I don't remember them until the late 1950s. I was riding with John Woodburn. We went into a café and there were mushrooms on the menu; we had to have them, it was a real treat."

Elthorne Road became Alf's stomping ground. He attended Acland Burghley School at Tufnell Park, a 15-minute walk up and across the Holloway Road. I'd heard rumours and read that Alf was expelled from school for disruptive behaviour on almost every conceivable level. It is a part of the myth, the early brush with authority, reacting to the dead hand of officialdom. Only in this case, it's not entirely true.

"There were three classes with over 40 in each class, and you took the 11-plus exam. Out of the three classes of 120 students, only four went forward to anything other than what was called a secondary modern school. Three of the four – their mothers were teachers. I took this spelling test; I'd never seen any of these words they were putting in front of me, and I didn't know the answers. I can't spell now, let alone then. By the time I got to the next school the teachers took an instant dislike to me. I can remember the Assistant Head saying to me: 'Empty vessels make the most noise'. The only reason they didn't throw me out straight away was that I won the running races and I won the swimming races. And at the end of the swimming races, the Headmaster, this big fat bloke, who had an Austin Ruby with a great concave seat in it from his weight, said, 'Well done Albert.' He couldn't even get my name right.

"There were other highlights from my time at school. When I was 12, during a lunch break, myself and two mates rode to Waterlow Park, about a mile away, to look at the goldfish in a pond. When we arrived there we noticed one of the ponds had been drained. Right in the margin of the pond I could see something, it was a rusty hand grenade. I was thrilled to find it. We took it back to school and proceeded to show everyone – the colour drained from the teacher's face and they promptly phoned for the police."

At the time, corporal punishment was commonplace in schools. In 1952, when Alf was 12, a national poll of teachers indicated 89%

in favour, even if they bemoaned the slow reduction in frequency, as people turned away from the rod, ruler or whatever was to hand. In my case, in 1984, it was the hand, with a Headteacher fond of slapping us really hard with an open palm across the back of the legs. It bloody hurt. The cane was mythical by then, the nuclear option, but less so when Alf was 13, when seemingly minor transgressions carried savage consequences.

"The teachers used to hit us for stepping out of line. Whilst queuing up at school to have an immunisation injection I noticed that the boy in front of me was looking rather pale. Seizing the moment I said, 'Did you see that – the needle went right through that boy's arm.' He promptly fainted and I got a clip round the ear for causing yet more trouble."

Slowly, inevitably, education was creeping out of the Victorian era: by 1957 the Ministry of Education would be noting that it saw a school 'no longer as a machine for giving lessons but as a social unit concerned with the all-round development of boys and girls.'[3] But like disc brakes or tri-bars, these newfangled ideas took some time to trickle down to inner London.

"The Acland colours were gold and black, a barred tie, and I had a black waistcoat which wasn't school wear, with pearly buttons. The assistant head said I looked like a penguin, and that became my nickname at school. I didn't get expelled, but I couldn't go to school anyway because I wasn't welcome and was working. So whatever education I had was finished at 11 years old, and after that – nothing. I have since met people from the same school and they all felt they learnt nothing, even learned people, professors and the like. I always thought I was going to be a racer so it wasn't important."

Lesson 2

Cycle Speedway is good for getting girls

The post-war landscape in London provided an unlikely first taste of competitive cycling for the young Alf. The damaged city consisted of rubble marked by oddly untouched houses, each one standing awkwardly: a capped tooth in a row of rotten gaps and nothingness. The signs are still there today in the pockmarked façade of listing buildings, abruptly curtailed terraces, ghostly greens where there were once rectangles of houses. London in the early 1950s became a juxtaposition of open spaces and dereliction. Empty and unreconstructed bombsites became places of play, an adventure to children growing up in the gap-toothed maw of urban chaos and destruction.

My dad, born in Hammersmith in 1947, talks of visiting the city in the early 1950s, travelling from north to south, down from Dunstable (where his family ended up as farm labourers after grandfather was demobbed from the Royal Marine Commandos) heading to see an aunt in Tooting. His journey bisected the capital on the Northern Line; each time the train lumbered to the surface he caught a glimpse of the suburbs and a wounded city, heard the whirling sounds of reconstruction and saw angular cranes sketching serrated Xs on the skyline, suturing the deep wounds.

Wastelands and empty buildings make the best playgrounds, as every child knows. One where the imagination runs away and flirts with chaos, a blank canvas of the mind. In amongst the brick and cinder, a youth craze erupted in the early 1950s, that of cycle speedway. It's a straightforward discipline: lethal laps of a tiny oval cinder or gravel track on brakeless beaters. The growth in the sport was exponential, at least in part due to the ready availability of tracks and the low cost involved. According to contemporary reports, all you needed was a length of rope, some knicker elastic for the start and a job lot of 'clunkers' – the kind of slightly dilapidated bike that you thrash about on and leave anywhere because it would never get stolen.

Within a year of the end of hostilities, a national league and control board emerged. The bomb-sites were levelled off through manpower alone, bricks and batten marked the periphery of the loop. By 1950 the British Cycle Speedway Federation was up and running, led by Derek Bacon and Vic Cowell. Some of the early riders made the eventual leap into motorised speedway, others into cycling. The motorised version was alluring, with its roar and dust and filth at Stamford Bridge or Wimbledon, pre-war haunts of the motorbike riders drifting round and round in sprayed circles, as described by Len Finch: 'You'd go round and round with your left leg out, racing against each other. We all wanted to be motor-speedway riders when we grew up, so I suppose we were aping them.'[4] They wanted to be Ivan Mauger, Bill Kitchen or later on Peter Craven*, Teddy-boy quiff intact, a picture of boyish charm, until wearing the outfit with tabard, club symbol on the front, bike at an impossible angle, a mist of dirt accompanying the effortless drift.

It wasn't solely a London phenomenon, with Bristol alone boasting in excess of 30 teams. However, the numbers in London were enormous, with nearly 400 speedway outfits doing battle across the capital, each with a fantastic name and electrifying tabard design: Atoms, Monarchs, Pirates, Rockets, Flyers, Stars, Lions, Vampires, Aces. It caught the eye of Pathé News, looking to document a new social phenomenon:

> Just be aware of the new sport: daredevil cockney kids are using the blitzed terrain of Wellby church, New Cross, for a changing room. They are the gladiators of cycle speedway, aged between three and eighteen, and their dream is one day to ride the great dirt track wearing the colours of the local speedway team. It's only a bombsite, a bunch of kids having fun, but here's where the stars of speed are born. Sit back and see if you can spot a champion of tomorrow. It's tough on riders, the bill for shoe repairs![5]

---

* Craven started racing in 1949 at Stanley Road, Liverpool. He became a multiple world champion, winning his second world title in 1962 at Wembley in front of 62,000 fans. He died a year later, aged 29, at Meadowbank after hitting a fence.

The short clip provides a vivid insight into a markedly different era: the Church is an empty ruin, half-bricked up on its sides, with exposed lintels. The youngsters proudly pull on the tabards and a tin-pot helmet. The arena is nothing but dust, an uneven sea of cruel clinker and gravel, sloping away to follow the contours of the craters left by the *Luftwaffe*. Youngsters crowd the untopped walls and encroach on the track as corners become prime spots for crashes, a jack-knife of the long-raked bike. Braking is with the left leg, hugging the interior: 'nerves of iron and wrists of steel are what you want for the cycle speedway'.

Look closely at the riders and any one of them could be a young Alf Engers. His motives though might be questioned. "I was 14. Cycle Speedway is good for girls, and I went out with one of the other bloke's sisters." The lure of the opposite sex was the catalyst for reckless riding, in small circles, on a sit-up-and-beg.

"I can remember Horbush Hammers, Tottenham Kangaroos, Stepney Pirates, Warwick Lions. Archway Stars was us. Looking back at the photos you see these blokes watching in suits, with a big lapel. That would have been mid 1950s. We all had rubbish bikes with a long wheelbase and a huge rake on the fork. It was all cinder tracks and got very busy. There wasn't the entertainment around then, this was just prior to the age of television, not many people had sets, so to go out and watch a spectacle was bloody good. It was fun. In total contrast, this bloody television was like the stage, you opened these doors and there it was, this flickering thing in the corner of the room commanding attention. BBC announcers like McDonald Hobley would appear in the room. We were told that his black suit was actually dark green because the cameras can't cope with colours. All of that was to come."

It's the stuff of smoke and mirrors, of social change and the beady eye of the box in the corner beginning to change and shape our subjectivity. We see ourselves differently now, embracing the all-seeing eye. We do less cycle speedway.

"You'd see people on an old girl's bike, a step-through, that was the way to do it; cowhorns didn't work – you needed narrow bars. There were loads of these bomb-sites. When we started to go about some of the other teams had specialist bikes. It was actually a cycle dealer –

Wally Green – who started that. This was getting pretty serious. We just had old bikes, anything we could find, and then when we went away to ride against somebody like Barkingside Pirates, they had a coach, they had these special bikes, and they were match racing, cycle speedway, like sprinters would do now. That was quite something for us."

The first track for Alf was at the Nag's Head, on the apex of the Caledonian Road and Holloway Road. It was a bomb-site and is where the Archway Stars started out. Now, it's post-war housing, with the Old King's Head sitting between rows of modern awkwardness, post-war and then more post-war, post-post-war buildings, less and less brick, and more steel, more glass: the archetypal London layers of change and accretion.

"Back then, there was nothing, just bloody bricks everywhere, and dust and timber. The main thing I remember from the Nag's Head was we saw a kid throwing bricks at a wasps' nest – they all came out and covered this kid from head to toe. Fortunately, a policeman was nearby and he heard the commotion. He lit a newspaper, and went over to this kid and waved it around him. Luckily he didn't suffer too many stings in the end.

"Trevor Smith, who rode for Wally Green, made the super dirt-track bikes and then went on to make road bikes. He had a cycle shop. He sponsored an independent road team in the Edgware area and began to make specialist speedway frames: if you had a crash there was a thing supposed to stop the forks from going backwards. It didn't do a lot." In pictures you can see the bracing, a bodge job of thin metalwork reminiscent of a stayer with supported handlebars; but these were proper frankenbikes with bracing to stop everything folding in half under the savage forces of physics and angry teenagers.

Alf talks warmly of a key figure in the scene, with a suitably comic book nickname. The first supportive figure of many: 'Mad Bill Hurst', a piratical character with one purpose in life – getting the kids racing round a tiny dirt track at high speeds.

"Me and me mate were just riding round the track and this chap came up, in his twenties. We were kids. There was a clear age-gap which made him noticeable. It was Mad Bill Hurst and he said he was getting this team together of two or three local lads. He acquired this ancient lorry to travel about to the London suburbs, like Barkingside, taking on all the other teams. The thing chugged along at 20 miles an hour. On one occasion we were sitting on the tail-board, creeping around this roundabout and my foot must have had some 'twitch' and I think I might have 'accidentally' kicked somebody off the back. They were all quite horrified as he rolled off around the bend."

Before long, the Archway Stars inherited a track from Mad Bill Hurst at Stepney, a custom-made circle with a big fence around it, as speedway grew in stature and organisation. They used a large rope or a firehose (if one could be purloined), stuffed with sand to mark out the line. The tracks improved as time went on, with increasing resources and even some council support.

Sports historian Simon Inglis identified one of the driving reasons for the explosion of interest, passion, and rampant enthusiasm. 'It was the birth of a youth culture that hadn't existed before, which enabled kids to have a completely separate identity to their parents for the first time – cycle speedway was something that no adult did.'[6]

It was also a very British sport, a parochial form, a million miles away from the continental ideal. There is a lineation from this through to skiffle music, where the broken bike is analogous to the washboard and the tea-chest. It consists of distinctly DIY and low-key actions which are accessible, and can be traced through almost every youth movement in the UK, right up to Grime, although I strongly suspect I might be the first and last person to link cycle speedway with Dizzee Rascal. A quick browse through YouTube throws up a colour film from the 1950s: the Hellingly Lions taking on the Edmonton Saints. After eight years of bomb-site action, the council custom-built a track for the Edmonton outfit in a display of admirable largesse.

The speedway bubble gradually floated away on the breeze of post-war reconstruction, from the heyday of 10,000 vicarious spectators watching an international at the Empress Hall in Earls Court in 1950, to a fairly rapid decline throughout the decade. By the end of the 1950s, the boom had finished; National Service called up the most enthusiastic early adopters, whilst bomb-site clearance and rebuilding did for the rest, something Alf observed, "Gradually the sites were built over, until now, several times over, just like the old bakery in Copenhagen Street where we had the direct hit."

Speedway is still clinging on as a sport, with purpose-built tracks here and there; there are two in Norwich and even one at the Velodrome in Newport, where the 1950s have yet to come to a definitive end, but it has slipped into the margins of cycle-sport within the UK. It is an anachronism that resists the contemporary trend for things being lighter, faster, more slippery and more expensive. Nevertheless, it was a compelling and rebellious first taste of competitive cycling for Alf, an elbows-out affair of conflict, rivalry, and a thirst for success.

Lesson 3

We can't all be national champions

At school, Alf didn't ride, he ran. He was unbeaten in running races, whether sprints or middle distance. He had a bike for riding around on, but it weighed 45lbs on the baker's scales. He used to get skinned regularly by his peers when out on 'tear-ups'. Despite this, the lure of the bicycle proved strong and Alf joined the Barnet Cycling Cub in 1952, aged twelve, at least in part due to a kindly word of support from Connie Charlton, *née* Stubbs: 'I must be the only woman ever to catch Alfie Engers. I was riding up Hornsey Rise when I drew level with a very young lad. He told me his name, said he worked in a bakery and was thinking of joining a club...' and thus he joined the Barnet*. Even then, he was still passionate about running and looked to the athletics track for his heroes. But in parallel with his running, Alf began to ride more.

His membership of the Barnet opened up a full diet of club runs, evening 10- and 25-mile time trials hosted by clubs, formal open events and road races. The club runs were long, all-day affairs, a test of endurance: "We'd go out most of the day and, it being Sunday, all the cafes were closed. Late on in one ride it became apparent someone had a six-penny bar of chocolate. It went for 10 shillings."

Being in the club led to an increase in speed and a rapid accumulation of experience over a short period of time. As the allure of speedway began to dissipate it was replaced with a fascination for the continental style of massed-start races, with nearby Finsbury Park being the epicentre of bike racing in North London. Alan Steer used to ride with Alf: "I can't quite remember how we came to join the Barnet. I guess it was one of the more attractive clubs, with Ted Gerard and Alan Shorter [more on these two later]. We would meet in a room above a pub in Barnet High Street. The London boundary finished

---

* This account is reported in Tim Hilton's *One More Kilometre and We're in the Showers*.

27

under the Archway bridge (where Islington met Hornsey and London met Hertfordshire) causing a straight line where two different types of tarmac met. It became a mark of honour among our group of lads to be the first one to sprint over the line when returning from club night. Probably my only claim to fame is being one of the few people to beat Alf in a sprint."

Alf was intoxicated by images of the riders of the era: "It was all about Fausto Coppi, *Il Campionissimo*. I used to cycle down to Leicester Square, there was this Mews and a stationer's shop where they sold *Le Miroir des Sports* and I collected the magazines. Time trialling didn't interest me, I wanted to be a road man, or a track man." There wasn't really any road racing to speak of, it was primarily circuit races, either in towns and city centre parks – Victoria Park in Bath was a popular loop – or at any of the huge number of post-war aerodromes: Matching Green, Dunmow, Stapleford Tawney. The conventional view of Alf is one of a single interest: the time trial, but that ignores both his roots in cycling and a steady diet of road races over the years. It's entertaining to see how little the young Alf cared for racing against the clock.

At this point three important people appeared in Alf Enger's life: Alan Shorter, Len Thorpe and Ted Gerrard. Their names resurface time and time again – a formative influence and a guiding hand throughout the years. All three merit a picaresque novel in their own right, one that treads a thin line between amazing stories of camaraderie and support, grass-roots cycling, élite championship road racing, and the salacious and, at times, controversial delights of a life outside of cycling. In the interim, Alan Shorter, or 'Old Al' as Alf affectionately calls him, took Alf under his wing, as he would do with many other young cyclists in the Barnet. Shorter's cycling career had been curtailed by injury after twenty years and he looked instead to coach and support the next generation. He became an important figure for Alf, who would later declare, "My successes were Al's successes".

"Old Al used to take me to races to watch Ted Gerrard. We would watch him preparing. Ted was already national road champion and his meticulous preparation of everything left a big impression on me. Ted had a track bike which weighed 12.5lbs [a ridiculous 5.7kg] which was far lighter than anything I had ever seen. I wanted to race, and was encouraged to do so. I wasn't particularly keen on time trials and longed to ride the massed-start races. The problem was that you had to be 16 years old, so I lied about my age."

Despite his preference for the road, Alf also began competing in 25-mile time trials, making his debut in 1952 at the Bignall's Corner course between London and Hatfield. He opted for derailleur gears and clocked 1-12, before being informed by his clubmates and co-competitors that variable gears added at least two minutes on to his time. It would be nearly a decade before John Woodburn broke the hegemony of the fixed-wheel bicycle. It was probably the first and last time Alf Engers was instructed on his equipment choices by other people. A year later, in 1953, at the London Clarion longmarkers event, he was fourth in 1-07-05. He then nudged under the hour, using a 78" gear. "I think I was number 9. I had cardboard in the shoe to prevent the tintacks impaling my feet. It was won by Eric Beecham and I felt I was on the road to becoming a racer." To break 'evens' at the age of thirteen was a startling achievement. At the time, the competition record of 56-24 had been set by Stan Higginson, one of the twins who redefined time trialling in the early 1950s with their fluidity and *souplesse*. They made their mark on the young Alf.

"I saw the Higginson twins in action on the F1 in a national championship. Their whole-hearted approach to cycling was my first turn-on for any branch of the sport. Their preparation, appearance, style of riding, the line they took on the road... they used to ride in a dead straight line, no messing, straight corners. They became my heroes. I can remember getting some pictures of them from Len Thorpe. I studied their positions, tried to emulate their style, which of course was later to get me into a lot of trouble with the governing body.

"They used to take the ball bearings out of their wheels and bottom brackets and polish them. One of them had spun the wheels before they went on a coffee break and a quarter of an hour later they were still turning round. I was very impressed with the way they rode, they were rock steady and you could have balanced a glass of water on their back. Later, I spoke to Bernard Higginson at the Skol Six and told him, 'You got me into trouble by your way of riding.' That was how you rode, in straight lines; there wasn't any traffic on the road. The only traffic was usually fishermen who were going to cast their nets. You could ride in straight lines rather than curves: it's a shorter distance. You could steal a march." As well as pictures of the Higginson twins, Alf covered his bedroom wall with a gallery of short-distance cycling stars, getting the photos from Len Thorpe. "People who were going well, I stuck them on the wall. I had Norman Sheil, Ray Hutchins, Joe Walley, all the current 25-milers at the time. They had an event called the Solihull invitation – the week before the National '25' – it had the form guide in the Comic. I'd take them down once I'd beaten them – *there's another one.*"

Throughout the early and mid 1950s, Alf's hero was Sir Roger Bannister, despite his fascination and growing passion for cycling. The peerless runner's epochal four-minute mile in 1954 cast a spell, and Bannister's description of the race helps to explain why:

I slipped in behind Brasher, feeling tremendously full of running, my legs seemed to meet almost no resistance at all, almost as though impelled by an unknown force. Brasher could have run the first lap in 55 seconds and I wouldn't have noticed.

Crowds stood on the banks above the Iffley Road track; a hubbub and excitement in expectation that something special might be about to happen. The noise swells midway through the lap and applause starts as they pass the half-mile in 1-58.

I was relaxing so much that my mind seemed almost detached from my body. It was incredible that we could run at this speed without strain.

I had to run the last lap in 59 seconds. Chataway led and I pounced past, 300 yards to the finish. I had a moment of mixed joy and anger and then my mind took over, it raced well ahead of my body and drew me compellingly forward. I felt that the moment of a lifetime had come. Those last few seconds seemed never-ending. The faint line of the finishing tape stood ahead as a haven of peace after the struggle. I leapt at the tape, like a man taking his last spring. My effort was over and I collapsed almost unconscious with an arm on either side of me. It was only then that the real pain overtook me. I knew I had done it.[7]

There are many parallels with Alf's later races in that description of intense effort and a state of grace, but in these early years it was simply a source of inspiration. Alf always wanted to meet Bannister, but it never happened. "I met Herb Elliott [the famous Australian and Olympic 1,500m Champion]; it was one of these things at the Albert Hall and the only thing I can remember is that he looked small to me, and he had dandruff on his suit, you could see it in the lights."

Alf was also captivated by the performances of Ray Booty throughout the mid 1950s, as he edged closer to the mythical four-hour 100. Ray Booty in full flight is a joyous spectacle; whether it's illuminating the BCF Championships in 1959 or hammering up Stanford Bank, all 6' 4" of him. In grainy cine footage from the era, there is a sense of sheer strength and grace working somehow in tandem.

Al Shorter took Alf to the Bath Road 100 in 1956, whilst Len Thorpe made his own way there in his 'shooting brake'.* Somehow Alf managed to combine three of his favourite things – fishing, practical jokes and cycling – in one exciting excursion.

"There's a track; you can't get a car down there, but we walked down and we'd had a couple of pints of lager and lime, and on the way back there was Thorpey's car with Thorpey asleep just waiting for the morning. We looked in the car and could see this alarm clock on the dashboard. We shook the car back and forth and he shot out like a bullet out of a gun, if he'd got hold of us he'd have killed us.

"That morning we poached from the stream; gave a couple to the Boot. Years later I met Eileen Sheridan, she knew Booty's girlfriend who told Eileen the story, including how she had actually filleted these things. Anyway, I think we were in Newbury, and old Al was looking at his watch and he said, 'If he's going to do it he's got to come along now,' and he suddenly appeared out of the morning mist. It was

---

*I had to ask Alf what a shooting brake was. He looked at me askance, as though I'd become diminished slightly by not having the faintest idea what he was talking about.

amazing to see this bloke going down the road refusing all drinks, and everything. It was a memorable moment in my cycling life, to be there when it actually happened."

There is a certain symmetry between the two achievements; four minutes for Bannister, four hours for Booty. It is a mark that can no longer be beaten, insofar as only one person will ever manage the first 25-miles-per-hour '100'. All other records are somehow less significant, or memorable, because of our obsession with fixed marks and even numbers.

Things move on, to the extent that the first 30mph '100' was recently achieved. It's best to ignore Richard Bideau's traumatic experience when, in 2015, he seemed to have become the first to achieve that mark, only for the course to be re-measured and declared 350 yards short of 100 miles. It is the 'roundness' of such records that lends itself well to memory; and I suspect that the young Alf knew a benchmark when he saw one, and imagined in the early morning that one day he might be able to achieve something similar, be helped from the bike by a crowd of awestruck well-wishers and bask in the collective glory of the sport.

Alf made steady progress and his peers at the Barnet saw something special in the charismatic teenager. There was the baking, the work for Alf Senior in Archway, the late nights and early mornings, and then there was cycling, increasingly becoming the most important thing in his life and steadily usurping the running. On the way back from an evening '10' in 1954 everything came perilously close to becoming unstuck, permanently.

"I was riding south towards Archway. I had wheels on the front carrier and had just done a personal best. Things were going well, I'd won a couple of road races, including my first circuit at Stapleford Tawney, and I finished in the top three regularly. I was coming away from this set of traffic lights north of Suicide Bridge*. I had my head down, thinking what I was going to do at the weekend and beyond; my target was the National Junior Championships at the weekend and I thought I was in with a shout. I was dreaming of the race, of my big effort. The next thing I knew I was flying through the air.

---

* Hornsey Lane Bridge, known as Suicide Bridge, for obvious and tragic reasons.

"A group from the North London CC called an ambulance and one of the riders notified my parents. Lying in casualty, I was shown the X-Ray of my kneecap; it had been totally shattered into pieces by the impact. It was a mess, just bits. I asked the doctor if he thought it'd be OK for the weekend; he said it might take a bit longer. I was in hospital for six weeks. They repaired it by removing the bits and tying it together with the ligament. I had to gradually stretch it; the physio said I should do six times up Highgate Hill to exercise it. I gradually got more flex and had to put the saddle right up. Fortunately, I never thought it would be the end; it was just something to be got through. In hindsight I know how lucky I was."

Within a year Alf was back riding and racing, somehow overcoming a career-threatening injury with barely a pause for breath. 1956 was a breakthrough year, enough to make 'Junior Corner' in *Cycling* in 1957, as he chased the Junior National title. He took the British League of Racing Cyclists (BLRC) North London and the National Cyclists' Union (NCU) London Centre titles, before lining up for the NCU National Junior Championships. Engers was full of confidence, having scalped Dennis Tarr earlier on in the season. Tarr was the NCU champion in 1955, before going on to have a successful career as a professional, riding for Condor Mackeson and Witcomb. The championship race took place at Church Lawford, a Second World War aerodrome not far from Rugby. The marked men in the field were Jim George and Ken Haddon.

"I remember it vividly. I was feeling dog rough, to the extent that I kept trying to put my gear into the wheel so I could climb off. I never got on with the heat. I think I was taking salt tablets because that's what the chemist told me to take; it was probably the worst thing because you'll get dehydrated. The course consisted of a straight, an uphill with a hairpin and then a downhill. Jim George's mother went up from the finish and as he came through on the last lap she practically patted him on the back and said, 'Yes you've got it,' and I thought, 'Yeah, I'll pat him on the back too.' I said, 'You can do it, Jim,' and he said, 'There's this bloke here, Ken Haddon,' and I said, 'Nah, you can beat him.' And we got down onto this straight, and I've never played sprinters before, not on the road, and they started this business behind me, looking and looking and looking. All of a sudden he jumped and I stamped on the pedals in response, and he didn't get by. It was so close.

"Thinking back, that really did go to my head. I felt like I would have won the year previously as well. After the accident I was just glad to be riding again. It took a long time for my legs to be the same size; the right was two and a half inches thinner. I took the NCU jersey and medal home to show my parents. They both sat there and said nothing. It seemed as if they didn't know what to say. In the end, I said, 'That's good isn't it?' And my father looked up, said, 'Yes.' Then he looked down again and rolled himself a cigarette.

"Once you've got that jersey, the junior bands, you're a marked man. Riding on the road I remember somebody went for a prime, and I easily got up to him, and this bloke threw his bike at me; we both ended up on the ground, and I've still got the marks now. I said, 'What did you want to do that for, mate?' And he said, 'Well, we can't all be national champions'."

Lesson 4

Most people seem to only want to know you for what they can screw you for

One of the first challenges in any conversation with Alf Engers is how to untangle the complex web of interconnected people within the North London club scene. At times, it feels like a nineteenth-century Russian novel. His asides are peppered with oblique references to the 'North London Mafia'. Groups of riders, tradesmen and clubmen, all orbit like quarks and hadrons, existing but only in relative terms, springing into life through collisions before disappearing again into the void. It's absurdly complicated, often very funny and vaguely salacious, making it a challenge to get it down on paper. The narrative is underscored and lightened by an array of nicknames and *noms-de-plume* which seem to shift and change: Old Al, Engerselli, Gerrardo, Eddie the Greek, Mad Bill, coalescing to form a cast from a Guy Ritchie film, only much more surreal, far funnier, and infinitely more confusing.

In short, the North London cycling scene was a convoluted mass of self-employed bike sellers, tubular repairers, clubmen and women, and other assorted people, all with a connection to the world of bicycles. It was an octopus with multiples of eight tentacles, eight squared, to the power of confused. The tentacles reach out to grasp hold of Ken and Alec Bird, Clive and Stuart Biddulph of Clive Stuart Cycles, Nicolino D'Alessandro, Solley Fellman, Alan Rochford, and the Braysher Brothers. This doesn't include the riders, most of whom were called John or Mick. From within this scene, three members of the Barnet Cycling Club emerge as catalysts to this story: Alan Shorter, Len Thorpe and Ted Gerrard.

Alan Shorter met Alf at Finsbury Park in the very early 1950s, watching the massed-start races. He was looking for a promising youngster to coach, and Alf more than fitted the description. It's tempting, and probably accurate, to frame the relationship as a *de facto* father-son relationship, filling a tangible absence for Alf: it was positive, nurturing and warm. They then travelled, together with others from the Barnet CC, to watch and participate in races.

"We would cram into the shooting brake,* and when we went round the corner the suspension would touch the wheel off so we all had to move round to the other side to stop it. It was keeling over. For the next step up, Old Al bought a brand new van. Back then you could buy a standard van without any paint and it was a couple of hundred pounds cheaper. It was always going to get painted but somehow it never did. A year after that he managed to buy this Ford Zodiac, which was really several steps up; it was this red and black thing. Old Al had never been a hundred miles an hour in a car before. We'd been to a race on the F1, and there was a long downhill stretch and he said, 'It's a hundred now,' at which point the bonnet catch went and flicked right up. I screamed, 'AL, THE BONNET!' and he took his foot off and very carefully slowed down. If that had come up, it would have been that."

Whilst Alf continued to work as an apprentice confectioner for his father at the bakery in Archway, he began to run errands for Solley Fellman, who imported Urago bikes and Clement tyres to his shop in Warren Street. Alan Shorter repaired tubular tyres for Fellman in a Mews just off Grays Inn Road, not far from Condor Cycles. He shared the mews with Nicolino D'Allessandro who sold the tubulars in the first place. It was quite a cottage industry, and Alf began shuttling between Fellman and Shorter. "I'd go with a big haversack and take the repaired tyres a mile or so away to Solley Fellman, and collect a new lot. I'd help repair them all, then bring them back." The rent was expensive for Shorter, coming in at nine pounds per week. Fortuitously, there was an empty flat at the top of the bakery which Engers senior was persuaded to let to Shorter for three pounds a week instead. Meanwhile, Fellman's business collapsed in the face of competition from nearby frame builders and cycle dealers, and a problem with 'evaporating' stock.

Alan Shorter then took on the lease of an empty shop at Elthorne Road, a stone's throw from the bakery. Alf is unequivocal about

---

* What's a shooting brake? You youngsters! An old estate car with wooden bits. Sometimes called a Traveller or Clubman.

the influence of Alan Shorter: "He helped me in cycling more than anybody else. He helped everybody. As a person he was kind and knowledgeable. I remember somebody saying to him, 'You're a has-been'. Old Al replied, 'Better to be a has-been than a never-was or never-going-to-be'."

Alongside Shorter, the other key figure in Alf's formative years was Ted Gerrard, also of the Barnet Cycling Club. Gerrard was an accomplished roadman who won the National Road Championship when he was 19 years old, beating Bernard Pusey and Fred Krebs, who both went on to ride the Tour de France in 1955 for the GB national team. He worked for Monty Young, founder of Condor Cycles, in the Grays Inn Road shop. He left Condor Cycles in 1956 to set up in Woodhouse Road, East Finchley, and took Tom Braysher, one of the Condor frame builders, with him. Gerrard was an entrepreneur, with many fingers in many different pies. His canny idea was to market bike 'kits' to avoid paying tax, sending the frames out in boxes minus the handlebars. It worked a treat and his adverts are emblazoned throughout Cycling in the 1950s. He had a good run of it, until things got a bit grippy in the early 1960s. A string of poor choices and unwise investments led to an investigation from the fraud squad and a spell in prison. The Woodhouse Road shop passed across to Alan Shorter, who took on the 'Gerrard Empire'. On his release from prison Gerrard found that most of his previous holdings had gone. He then worked for his father, a taxidermist in Camden Town, and began importing fur rugs, which in turn led to another complex series of events involving bonded warehouses, break-ins and the like, and a second spell at Her Majesty's Pleasure. Since then, Gerrard has been living on Pabay, an island off the coast of Skye, and has published philosophical books about birds and Aristotle.

Len Thorpe was the third member of the triumvirate and the only one not directly involved in the cycle trade, but he did have an illustrious background as a top-level tester, which included holding the competition record at 50 miles from 1937 until 1946. He rode a Bates Cantiflex at the time – a slightly strange bike with an 'S' bend front fork.* Thorpe was a lifelong member of the Barnet CC and a

---

* Like Hetchins, having a unique frame design helped with brand recognition.

professional photographer responsible for some of the seminal images of time trialling in the 1950s and 1960s. Engers speaks fondly of Thorpe, or 'Thorpey' as he was known, but doesn't shy away from painting him as a caricature, someone with more than a whiff of Benny Hill about him, variously described as a 'robust and naughty bloke' by others who knew him. "You always knew where you stood with Len Thorpe because he would always let you down. He was a photographer and he had these blue films. There were several members of the Barnet that made front page of *The People* and there are not that many clubs that can boast of that. He was set up by *The People*: he did these stag shows and *The People* had been to a couple of them and the police got to know about it. The reporter said, 'Unless you give us a few pictures of you creeping away, we're going to tell whoever it is about all these other film shows you've done.' So there was a picture of Len Thorpe by his car, with the number plate clearly visible, creeping away with these big film cans under his arm and it said: 'LEN THORPE: THE VILE PURVEYOR OF FILTH'."

"There was a great camaraderie; the Barnett was a great club, full of characters."

Lesson 5

Cycling is a reason to live

"You had a reason to exist, practically. Racing and training was everything. We met up of an evening at the Marshmoor Café just outside of Hatfield, rode around then had a tear-up back. Maybe 20 or 30 of us would do the Hertfordshire loop. The same existed in London where we would use the Regent's Park outer circle. The testers would take on the roadmen. There'd be the shout of 'Up the League', with the reply, 'Fuck the League'. There were all these signs in the cafe, 'No cyclists served'. There was a hooligan element, an outsider bit to it, particularly with the Highgate CC. They had a list of ten things to do on Guy Fawkes Night, number ten was to sling a firework into a policeman's car. Graham Vines* out of the Highgate got all ten.

"It has dissipated now, that scene. The inter-clubs were electric affairs, the one at Ealing Manor was ferociously fought. The club dinner at the end of the year, that was like the BAR concert used to be, everybody together, discussing whatever. I was always thinking, 'Christ, what about next year?' It was a reason to live."

The Marshmoor was a haunt of many cycling clubs, the tearoom of choice for day-long club runs and an established meeting place. Finsbury Park CC would head out to the café and back on Wednesday evenings, and the Marshmoor features in the almanacs of almost all North London clubs of the time, including the Northwood Wheelers:

> After this we went to the Havelock café, then home. I then went out with Roger Bingham to dinner with the club at the 'Shanty' at Bourne End, where we met Stan and a friend of his. After dinner we went through Water End, Hemel Hempstead, Leverstock Green and St Albans to the Marshmoor café for tea. Met the rest of the club here, and afterwards we came home the usual way through Radlett, Aldenham and Watford. A very nice day.[8]

---

* NCU Champion in 1951, and professional champion in 1955

The Marshmoor, Christmas Day, 1952

Things have changed. The Marshmoor has gone. Everything about time trialling now is different, which is inevitable. In many ways it is barely recognisable as the same sporting endeavour, but in others it is fundamentally unchanged. It remains uniquely British as a major sporting hobby, defining amateur cycling within the UK. It is everything else that has changed and, with it, the sport of cycling has shifted.

For Alf and his partners in time and place, there was an enviable sense of space: traffic was sparse and roads were empty. The bike was an empowering object, and combined form and function beautifully. Move forwards in time and personal mobility is no longer restrictive. People who ride long distances are cranks, not heroes, and the cosseted warmth of the car is preferable to the elemental exposure of the bicycle.

Nevertheless, clubs still exist and are growing in popularity, and both time trialling and road racing are more popular than ever: the leisure-orientated bike boom has drawn huge numbers to sportive and organised leisure riding, but the camaraderie and the fellowship of the road that Alf speaks of still exists, albeit within a broader and altered landscape. At times, club life seems to be subsumed beneath a diffuse mixture of transient commercial teams, shop outfits, or placeless affiliations to a brand. The pursuit of time itself remains honest, but has become ever more esoteric, technological, and expensive. People drive to races, avoiding their locality if the courses are slow. It's tempting to see this as a disconnect between place and club and person, but it's also about the way we live now. We work far away, commute long distances, lead disenfranchised lives and make up for the void left by the absence of tangible community through endless virtual networks. And yet, in 50 years time people will find our absurd modernity, our technological virility, nothing more than a quaint anachronism, and doubtless in our dotage we will debate endlessly about which is more authentic, on whatever virtual cycling software we use: the digitised off-road, or the digitised on-road circuits.

"We'd go away for a '25', ride to some village, stay over, do the race. On one occasion we were put up in a cottage in Lowick, near Thrapston. There was an elderly lady, and there was no running water. You had to climb up this vertical ladder to the bedroom. This old lady said, 'The toilet is at the end of the garden but don't wear any perfume or the bees will attack you.' She prepared food; I didn't like it, but it was a sin not to eat it. I crept down to the garden, the toilet was perched on the end of the stream, I was anxious to avoid getting stung where it might hurt a lot. She told us a story about the vicar who also ran the library and used to siphon off half the money from the late library books. We were riding back home the next day and we saw the vicar riding a bike the other way with a library book under his arm and we all went 'WAHEEEYYY,' a proper cheer, and he looked confused and must have wondered what the bloody hell we were talking about.

"On another occasion we stayed in a barn. Woodburn got up with a jolt and legged it across the floor: a cat had got in and was clawing at his tubs. I've never seen him move so fast!"

By the late 1950s Alf's form was on the up. He was attaining a reputation as the fastest of the new breed and beginning to attract whispers of admiration. In 1958 he managed third in the Kettering RC promotion and he set his sights on the Championship '25' the following year. His form came good in May, with a win at the Colchester Rovers promotion by nearly a minute, prompting observers to speculate that he might win the championship, if the day was 'easy and fast'. This observation comes from Alf's relatively callow status: a simple out-and-back in good conditions would reward a younger rider, where pure speed might triumph over the experience and pacing needed on a lumpy, technical course with a growling headwind. It also marked the first time that Engers was referred to simply as 'Alf' in the press: 'Alf and Co. Wallop Champ' was the heading in the Comic, after reigning champion, Mick Ward, could only manage fourth. He was rapidly becoming known as 'Alf', with no other appellation necessary, such was his distinctive style, speed and character. It is a unique privilege not afforded to many other riders: no Brad, Chris or Pete. 'Cav' is arguably the closest, another wildly ferocious competitor with bags of charisma.

Hot favourite was Gordon Ian, the most consistent and stylish rider of the previous few years. He looked fantastic on a bike, and at 28 years old was taking on all-comers. The 'hope of the south' (a typical phrase deployed by *Cycling* at the time on account of the Northern hegemony) was Ken Craven. Past champions on the line included Mick Ward and Mike Gambrill, and the legendary Bill Holmes.*

It was ideal championship weather, a clement June day with vaguely drifting air, 'a day for maximum gearing' according to the Comic[9] but according to Alf, some 58 years later, it was always maximum gearing, day in day out, and it was always 86". Alf, just three days past his nineteenth birthday, was being tipped by the tifosi, after a win on the course just the week before. He looked lean and hungry; his angular features are unmistakable in photos from the day, as is the Barnet jersey, with thick bands around the arms, and he isn't wearing socks. A tiny wristwatch gives an indication of time, the rest is pure road and path: a spear-point lugged stem, single brake and half-taped bars, with a shallow rake on the fork and pencil stays.

He went out hard, on five ounce tyres and the 86" gear, and smashed it to the turn and back, before the last quarter started to bite, making it

---

* Bill Holmes raced in the 1956 and 1960 Olympics, winning a silver medal in the team time trial. He also won multiple Milk Race stages and the overall in 1961.

a struggle home. 'But what a glorious battle he put up' read the report in *Cycling*[10], getting out of the saddle on the incline and then hurtling along the straight, before a collapse on the grass verge, utterly spent, beyond spent, chasing oxygen that wasn't there. John Woodburn was well down in nineteenth. Alf had done enough for third, with 56-22 in a tight race, edged out by Ken Craven by 10 seconds and by Gordon Ian's superlative winning ride of 56-03. The first three riders all achieved a personal best. Alf's first podium placing in a championship race also heralded the first complaint against him, regarding accusations of a 'following car'. "It was actually the editor of *Cycling* and I didn't even know he was there." It was an ominous encounter.

From the very start, Alf seemed to exert a magnetism: his charismatic approach attracted admirers and detractors in equal measure. The parochial world of time trialling seemed ill-prepared for such things, and the turbulent wake that followed behind. In 1959 the sport was closely guarded, highly principled, and had emerged out of adversity: a ban on riding on the roads led to a secretive and Masonic approach, using code words and black alpaca clothing on the edge of town, at dawn. Lists of competitors and results were headed 'private and confidential'.

Where there are principles there is dogma. The RTTC came into being in 1922, formed by F.T. Bidlake. Take out the war years and it was barely thirty years old. There was a desire to sustain the values of the sport, to safeguard amateurism and foreground time trialling as the true discipline. The split between the NCU and RTTC was challenged by a lengthy treatise on the subject – 'The Council's Statement on the Menace of Mass Start Racing on the Highway':

> Bunched racing is an utterly selfish and irresponsible use of roads; the policy of the Council is that all such racing should be stopped; the ringleaders and their associates of the BLRC have only financial gain as their motive; unsuspecting commercial concerns and newspapers have been given a distorted story about road racing; BLRC road races violate every one of the principles of clean amateurism, authenticity, and regard for public safety. [11]

Even though they were ostensibly opposed to massed-start racing, the statement encompassed anything that might threaten the precarious status quo. The RTTC were the defenders of the light; crusaders for the common good. In this context, the high visibility of a rider like Alf, his defiance and bluster, acerbic wit and desire to do things his way, ruffled a few feathers right from the start, as did others in the Barnet, and elsewhere.

Over the course of the year Alf churned out a remarkable seventeen sub-58 minute rides, at that point seen as the benchmark for the really fast riders, and he was second only to Gordon Ian in the 'consistently rapid' bracket. He turned his hand to the track, riding regularly at Paddington, Herne Hill and elsewhere, including the brand new track at Welwyn Garden City, where he rode a 4-man training session with Mike Gambrill (Clarence Wheelers), John Woodburn and Robin Buchan (Norwood Paragon). It was the opening meeting for the track and Alf won the individual pursuit in 5-13 after going 'off like a bomb', replete in a white jersey and hairnet helmet with a white stripe down the middle, determined expression and cotton track mitts gripping the bars. It didn't go entirely smoothly. "The new track was tarmac and it was actually melting." Woodburn was second.

Beryl Burton was also racing that day, with a very young Denise with her. Alf mentions Beryl Burton often: "She is the best British female cyclist of all time. Sorry to all the others. She was that bloody strong. We stayed at her place for the team once. Her cat was there and we filled up saucers of milk and fed it scraps, then told Beryl we'd fed the cat – you know, helping out. She said, 'I haven't got a cat'."

Alf was sustaining his form, riding through from May to the end of the season, and he opted to close things out at the Leyton CRC 25-mile event. Both Alf and John Woodburn, at that point a Reading Wheeler, were down to ride the event. Alf opted for an 85.7" gear, whilst Woodburn flirted with variable gears, as he was wont to do at that time. The course went out and back on the Southend Road and was fast.

"I certainly remember that day. I wanted to do a long 55, what Norman Sheil was doing. He was a pursuiter and a pain in the arse. He was a strong rider, which was why he was a pain in the arse. But he was also a bit of a pain in the arse. I put it down to the North-South divide. If you were a southerner, then double thumbs down for you. Turning round in the road and coming back, it was quiet, and old Al was down the road and shouted to me. I pedalled so quickly and I got to the finish and back and old Al said, '55-14.' I refused to believe it. Al looked confused by the watch. I couldn't believe that I might have beaten Norman Sheil.* Someone else said, '55-12.' And I thought, 'Christ, it couldn't be that; I must be outside 55 but I had done a PB. They must have got it wrong and it was going to be corrected to a 56.' I wanted to do 55 minutes; he's saying '55-14' and looking puzzled. Then someone else said, 'The timekeeper says it's a 55-11,' and it began to sink in that maybe I'd broken the record. I get a lump in me throat even now. I went fishing straight away afterwards, and I got a picture of me, with me dog, sitting there. Fishing maybe is the saviour of it all."

Alf had lopped 27 seconds from the championship record and the next rider came in nearly two minutes back. It was his first big record ride, with the tantalising promise of much more to come. Where you might expect positive memories, a sense of lasting elation, it's clear there is a tumult of feeling swirling beneath the surface, not least of which is that even in the telling, Alf is welling up, pausing, and fighting the accumulated memories and awakening feelings from that year. It was a challenging time in many respects. His father died and he was living with his wife's parents, waiting to get married in October. The wedding photo even featured in *Cycling* – Alf in a high-lapelled suit and narrow tie, with a beaming smile, arm in arm with Janet, his wife.

The absence of a will led to his father's inheritance being contested and left Alf's mother without access to money; she pawned her wedding ring for a while. Alf felt unable to help and struggled to cope with the situation. He felt huge pressure to earn a living. But that's just scratching the surface. At home he didn't get help and he didn't get recognition of his achievements in terms of cycling. He is so hard to get to, even now. Maybe the years have insulated the memories against prying questions. Eventually, two years later, we get there.

---

* World Pursuit Champion, 1955 and '58, he rode the Tour in 1960 – an all-round hardman and much-respected racer.

"It was a small bakery. Dad always used to say, 'Who's going to look after this when I'm gone?' He implied it was me. I came back from another job, to help in the bakery; it wasn't making any money. I came home one day from work…"

A pause.

"I almost wish I hadn't started this."

A pause, an intake of breath. A silence comes creeping in.

"I've never told anyone this. He said, 'I'm selling the bakery.' I said, 'What am I going to do?' And he said, 'You can work for the people that buy it.' That was that. It was a rejection; he was saying, *bugger you*. So I wasn't speaking to him. It was in 1959, a matter of months before he died. He died in April. The story goes that I went to a race; he looked at the clock at eight on the Sunday morning, said, 'He's off.' And he had a cerebral haemorrhage and never came out of it. If I were a Muslim I'd say it was God's punishment.

"I was out in the cold, the bakery was being sold on to somebody; me mother was very upset. She'd lost her husband and the bakery. She said, 'You killed your father by arguing with him.'

"After that I knew I wasn't going to be living with me mother and I was going to get married. That's the complete story. The new people came in, said they didn't want me working at the bakery. I was out with nowhere to live, no job. I went to live with my fiancée at her parents' place and had to find a new job."

After years of struggling to establish a relationship with his father, struggling to gain recognition for anything, it was over. It left only burning anger, regret and bitterness. "I would never tell a lie or not follow through on any promise. At the time, I thought, 'Bugger you mate.' It's only years and years later, I thought, 'Bloody hell, you miserable sod.' Anything my kids have done I've always said, 'Well done,' whether it's work or anything at all."

Alf looks up and around the room, trying to dispel the force of memory. He focuses on an old photo taken immediately after his National Junior Championship win, with Alf on his bike with the winner's bouquet, and Alan Shorter's arm around him, guiding him through the crowd. Both are smiling broadly, sharing in the moment.

It is an image which contrasts sharply with his father's blunt 'Yes' and rolled cigarette. Within the wider context of an unceasing desire for recognition and support, Alan Shorter fulfilled a yearning need.

In the aftermath of his father's death, Alf had little option but to throw himself into his work. "I ended up working six days a week, twelve hours a day. By the time I got home I felt tired and just wanted to sit down. It's hard manual work. I was a pastry cook, a master baker, everything. I was doing the lot. I thought the more you learnt, the more intricate the pastries, chocolates and whatever, the more money you would make, but it's actually the reverse, in the end. Shortly after I got married, not only was I working those hours I was also going to night school twice a week to do a chocolatier course: sugar boiler, all the stuff. I'd go straight from work to Borough Polytechnic and come home around midnight. Take those two days out and all the other working days, I was going out in the pitch black after I'd got home, six o' clock at night. It's not really a level playing field with the likes of Woodburn and people who weren't working."

For Alf, work comes first. It did then and it does now. Cycling could not provide a viable alternative. Some years later, Graham Huck recalled getting the better of Alf in an evening event at Newark, with both carding 58s, but Huck's was that bit quicker. The difference was that Alf had worked through the night baking, and carried on, then driven up to Newark for the race. Come the weekend, rested and ready, Alf beat Huck by four minutes.

The conflict between professional, amateur and independent status hung heavily in the air, both as a decision for Alf to take, but also as a niggling issue of disparity: some were working and yet not working; others had independent means, or the nature of their employment meant that they could fit work around cycling, rather than the other way round. It felt unfair. Alf was giving serious thought to the shift towards professional status, using the intermediary stage of 'independent' to test the water. Theoretically, it afforded a way in – and a way out if things went wrong, or success was not forthcoming. Going fully professional was a big step, whereas the independent category offered a middle ground. Typically, independents would be sponsored, but without a formal professional team. The category was withdrawn in 1966.

Alf remained as an amateur through 1960, with his biggest success being the most complicated. John Woodburn, John Harvey and Alf lined up for the Antelope Road Club 3-up team time trial on 22 May. It was a fast event and held as an unofficial selection run between the Olympic 'A' and 'B' teams. The six Olympic hopefuls were Bill Holmes, Bryan Wilcher, Ken Laidlaw, Robin Buchan, Roger Wilkings and Jim Hinds. The writing was on the wall with the Barnet outfit having shorter '25' times than any of the six chosen men. Barnet started strongly, flying along the Southampton to Bournemouth road. The 'B' outfit hit trouble and dropped Wilkings early on. Time checks confirmed Barnet were 16 seconds up at the halfway point. Alf was spinning a 100" gear and the gap opened up further, until they stopped the clock at a definitive 27 second mauling of the Olympic 'A' outfit.

"Every time we got to a hill, somehow or other Woodburn was on the front, complaining, 'Why do I always get all the bloody hills?' I was chortling to myself." There is one further twist: "I punctured. There was no following car. I took a tourist's bike and finished on that. It was probably within 5 miles of the end."

The BCF excuses came thick and fast: 'the team should have some practical experience of riding together'; a 'great performance... considering the pre-race setbacks.'[12]

"In the immediate aftermath we thought: 'We won, we're going to Rome.' Although deep down I think we knew it would never happen because we knew the hierarchy. At the time it didn't seem overly important; we were just out having fun. It was after not being selected for 1960 that those doubts began to increase: your face had to fit. It happened on more than one occasion.

"For Rome, they went for Charlie McCoy, who went on to break the 25-mile record in 1961, Barry Hoban, Joe McClean and Billy Holmes, along with Mick Gambrill. It was already set in stone. Even before the selection, the three up north wanted to keep together and they did. The odds were against us really. In the National Pursuit Championship I had an unbelievable nine punctures, I wouldn't have continued. Firstly I punctured against Charlie McCoy, and this bloke said, 'He is obviously better than you, so why don't you concede?' So

I threw the bike away and said, 'No.' I think after the next puncture McCoy conceded, but by the time I got to the final I could hardly stand up. The tyres had to be taped on. I'm a kid, a baker earning £10 a week; tyres are £3 each. It was taped on the outside every six inches with insulation tape. Well, that's what you did; no time to stick it on, it would never hold. Norman Sheil had the same thing in the time trial round against Barry Hoban at Fallowfield and he rode himself stupid. I was second to Barry Hoban. In addition, the two Olympians wouldn't ride pursuit against us. They were Mick Gambrill and Robin Buchan, a trackie, his mate. Two lots of mates, and me coming in. If I got up on the track to get in on the string Mick would say, 'No... form your string over there.' After the Championship '25' he warned me off the track altogether, saying, 'Somebody fell off and broke their collar bone,' or 'Somebody got killed the other day.' He'd do absolutely everything, as much as he could, to discourage me. Eventually they conspired against me, saying I crouched too low and went through too fast. It was decided that I was bad for team morale and I was dropped, and they went on to put in an abysmal performance." Alf had the beating of both Gambrill and Billy Holmes in the 25-mile events and they knew it. It was dispiriting.

The battle between Gordon Ian and Alf continued through 1960. Ian had edged the early exchanges. At Newark Alf punctured, grabbed a wheel and lost a minute, coming third behind Woodburn and Ian. At Erewash the next day he lost by 16 seconds to Ian on a very fast course. It was delicately poised for the Championship, with Alf chasing his first title and Ian his third. Any sense of delicate poise was destroyed the minute Alf charged away from the start. He broke nine of the 24 spokes in his rear wheel. He re-centred it quickly, rode five miles, changed onto another Barnet rider's bike, then got back on his newly fixed original machine at the turn. It was a tall order and he finished eighteenth, leaving Ian with a convincing victory. Ian, to his credit, was the fastest rider of the year, and had also been snubbed for Olympic selection, despite being a proven pursuiter. It seemed a minor blip for Alf; the price you pay for fragile but super-fast equipment, finely tuned wheels and Clement 2s, and, at a youthful 20 years of age, he would surely win the Championship at some point soon.

In 1961 Alf barely rode. He waited, worked and measured his options. Woodburn won the '25' Championship with a landmark victory on variable gears, changing the face of time trialling forever. Alf finished in a lowly twelfth place, running low on motivation and struggling to make ends meet. It all seemed a long way from the rhetorical headline in the Comic 18 months earlier: 'Engers – Will he get to Rome?'

The season ended with a trip to the Royal Albert Hall for the Champions' Dinner. Along with the customary dancing horses and jugglers, the guest of honour was Jacques Anquetil. Harvey, Woodburn and Engers received the trophy for fastest team in the '25' Championship from the Tour de France champion.

In 1962 Alf took the plunge and became an independent. It meant no more time trials and the beginning of a commitment to a career as a professional cyclist. He made his way across to Belgium with his wife. It was a short-lived experiment: "I rode with Tommy Simpson at Herne Hill and he said, 'Sell up, come over now.' It was a Meeting of the Champions: me, Woodburn, Piet van der Lans, two Australian six day riders – Reg Arnold was one. Tommy must have been staying locally because he arrived at the gate with his wheels on his back, and a jobsworth said, 'Where's your ticket?' and he said, 'I'm Tom Simpson.' The guy said, 'I don't care who you are, you ain't got a ticket you're not coming in.' And he wasn't going to let him in, but someone heard it and finally they got him in.

"We had done all these bloody events, I remember asking Alan Shorter what gear we were going to ride behind the dernys and he said, 92" or 94" and I thought that wasn't too bad. Then I asked Tommy and he said, 'No we'll ride 104".' I hadn't been riding that much at all. Tommy and Barry Hoban had just ridden the Tour of Flanders. You can imagine what it felt like. Then it came onto the *News of the World* sprint; these two big blokes were rolling round, the crowd watching intently. Then Tommy noticed a mallard in the centre of the green. He had got my tracksuit on and he was stalking this mallard around the green. The crowd disregarded the sprint and started watching and cheering Tommy Simpson trying to catch this mallard. He didn't catch it. I dunno what it is with me and animals. One time I was racing in Yorkshire on a super day. It started in a gritty lane, and I damaged the tyre. At one point I even had to shoulder the bike and run through a traffic jam. At the end I was coming up to the finish and it was mayhem, there were people everywhere. I couldn't see the timekeepers. There was a bloody pig running round the middle of the road squealing with a big crowd trying to trap it.

"We stayed in Ghent, just down the road from Albert Beurick's Cafe Den Enghel.* The best placing I had was fourth and I was only there for a ruddy week. The wife didn't like it; she broke down in tears straight away, and it was raining all the time. She asked, 'Why did we have to come here?' That more or less cancelled staying abroad. It was a very difficult period. I wanted to be a Tour rider, but I had to earn a living, that's it. Living had to come first, full stop."

Not for the first time, there is a sense of regret, of missed opportunities and the fickle hand of fate dealing from a loaded deck. It imbues a heaviness of mood, a sombre reflection, and a knowingness of the sacrifices that some people make, the inner struggle to reconcile feelings, thoughts, and the realities of the outside world of work and family life, juxtaposed with the time and physical and mental energy required to excel on the bike. Alf mentions Gordon Ian, the other big time triallist of the late 1950s, and then goes on to talk about other cyclists he has known who have struggled.

"Gordon Ian could ride the track and the road. He was a quiet bloke and he suffered from depression from time to time, which certainly I have. It's surprising how many of the top level cyclists have struggled. Darryl Webster found it tough going. Graeme Obree is open about it in his book. There's more than a few. As I understood it, it's just your brain bogged down: it doesn't produce the things you need. I have an affinity with those people. It's something you can't explain, an awareness of somebody who has been to the edge and maybe gone over it."

Like Alf, Darryl Webster is open about the difficult times he has had, particularly since he stopped cycling: "The darkest periods led to suicide attempts and destructive relationships. During the intense

---

* Albert Beurick supported Tommy Simpson and they later became business partners.

51

years of being an élite athlete much of normal life passes you by. You simply don't have the time, inclination or concern to pay it much attention. Everything is geared towards preparing for and executing the next training session or race. My depression had other causes but it's also probable that my poor coping mechanisms were the result of not having had to deal with 'normality'." In just one of the many parallels between the two riders, he endured an abortive professional career on the continent, even if he did last 51 weeks longer than Alf.

It's not that Alf is a depressive character, far from it: he is charismatic, physically arresting, bold and colourful, but within the silences and the stern glances, the unsaid things, lurks a darkness and an introspection. The two things work in tandem, and in tension. The battle with external forces – the selection body; the authorities – seems matched by a battle to keep the internal forces in check and channel the energy elsewhere. In this case, it is into the pursuit of speed, despite the limitations of everything else. If his father did nothing else, he at least indirectly instilled a desire to work and provide, and a thirst for recognition.

In our conversation I mention T.S. Eliot, writing about Webster (not Darryl, but John): "He saw the skull beneath the skin." Alf's response is direct: "That sounds about right. Maybe you can explain things to me. Tell me where I went wrong. Where do you find contentment? It can be very difficult, the frame itself is skewed. I remember my mother saying, 'You're never happy.' Why should I be happy?

"I could be contented if I caught a record fish. I'd be content for a while."

Lesson 6

If you want to do something properly, you can't work at the same time

Turning independent was a calculated decision, a potential stepping stone to professional status and a chance to test the water, to see if it was feasible to make a living through bike racing. Whilst Belgium had proven a non-starter, the chances of domestic success were good: Alf was as quick as the current crop of professionals, at least in terms of straight-line speed. They admired his ability, and were anxious about it. He was supported by Ted Gerrard initially, and raced with John Woodburn and John Harvey as sponsored riders. The taciturn John Woodburn had also been on the receiving end of a rustication from the RTTC. In 1961 he went to the right of a 'keep left' sign in order to avoid a marshal's car, and a scree of gutter grit and gravel. He confirmed this when asked about it afterwards by an RTTC official. His win was struck out. It was the last straw, and compounded the feeling that nothing any of the Barnet riders could do would lead to national selection. Like Alf, he cut his losses. Woodburn had won the '25' that year and was seeking a new challenge.

Any notion that becoming independent might lead to a sudden change in circumstances was quickly dispelled. Alf knew what his commitments were. "I was still working. As far as I know most independents at that time were working; there might have been one or two who were living at home or with independent means. Originally, it was supposed to be a stepping stone – if you didn't like it you could turn back – but that changed and you had to apply to be reinstated.'

The constant theme is of a need to provide, a need to work, to make a living. In effect, nothing changed. Alf carried on working long shifts as a patissier, night and day work, and he carried on fitting his training around work. He was no longer able to ride RTTC events and had to make a go of it on the road. As a result, the diet of victories from time trials dried up overnight. He experienced some success during this time. The first race for the trio was the Chiltern Road Club 50-mile massed start on 14 March 1962. Harvey was fifth, Woodburn seventh and Alf tenth. However, in the following 18 month period Alf barely rode. He did come second to Doug Meekins* in the Tour of North Hertfordshire, and was second again to Dave Bedwell in the Tour of Belvoir. Bedwell was a part of the all-conquering Viking trade team at the time and coming to the end of an illustrious career, with National Road Race wins in 1951 and 1961, multiple stage wins in the Tour of Britain and a top ten in the Peace Race. Peter Ryalls was third, having ridden the Tour de France the year before.

Alf was mixing it up with the very best, riding long miles, arduous races, working extremely long hours and somehow still managing to be competitive, but at a cost. He struggled to reconcile the need and desire to work for a living with the challenges involved in making the step up to full-time professional status. The increased training load was incompatible with his working hours and the forces ranged against him became debilitating. The physical cost was then amplified when Ted Gerrard's business fell apart within the year amidst a cavalcade of scandal and a visit from the long arm of the law, leading to his backing for the riders being pulled. Alf raced on briefly with support from Alan Shorter, who became the tenant at the Woodhouse Road Shop, taking over Gerrard's establishment in light of his 'absence'. Shorter continued to support and nurture Alf's career. In 1962 Alf was still a fresh-faced youngster with huge potential. However, after eighteen months as an independent he was already contemplating a return to the amateur ranks.

"I wasn't really competing. I didn't have any money having just got married. We were offered our racing kit, a bonus to win and Ted was going to provide a car to drive us around and get to events, so that was it, that was the incentive. Harvey and I went in Ted's Jaguar along the M4 to see Woodburn. It was the first time I'd been 128mph in a car. At some stage or other Ted was offering a 100 mph trip in his car to anyone who bought a bike. That stopped when a car got cut in half on the motorway. We were hitting the big time," he adds, with a hefty dose of sarcasm.

---

* Another of several alumni of the Barnet who was supported by Alan Shorter.

The resources available and the rewards for taking the plunge were not enough. In hindsight, the pressure Alf placed on himself to work and to support his wife, to run the business and carry on with his craft, meant that the adventure was doomed from the start. Independent status was supposed to be a middle ground. It ended up being something and nothing.

"I was surprised I ever found the time to cycle, what with working, fishing, married life, later on the boy, running a bakery. But I guess it's the same problem: if you want to do something properly, you can't work at the same time."

There is a hint of regret, or perhaps bitterness in the comments. It isn't anger directed at those who had an alternative, more a sense that the odds were stacked against him from the very beginning. The obstacles faced by Alf in the pursuit of success were greater, perhaps, than those that others had to contend with, despite his talent and strength as a bike rider. Maybe there is also a sense of wistfulness at what might have been. The sight of other riders, no better or worse, achieving recognition and reward throughout the sixties, being a part of the circus of professional life, even within the UK – hitting up the roads and riding the extensive calendar of tough events was galling. For him, it was never going to happen.

As a part of the initial trio riding for Gerrard, John Woodburn experienced more success, moving on to ride for Falcon Cycles in 1963, riding to fourteenth place in the Peace Race later that year and coming second behind Albert Hitchen in the London–York race. He also rode for Moulton Cycles, managing to cover the 162 miles between London and Cardiff at an average speed of 24mph. On a Moulton! He was paid £1 per mile – a lot of money at the time – but a fantastic return in terms of the sales boost and credibility it gave the fledgling company. Even now they are a much-revered bike brand, except perhaps by Doug Collins who recalled riding one for the London–Holyhead, as a part of the marketing strategy for the brand. He was tacking along absolutely fine, until it collapsed beneath him.

In later years Woodburn reinvented himself as the archetypal Super-Vet and long-distance bike rider, redefining age-group records and competing with the young bucks head-on. His famous end-to-end record of 45 hours, 3 minutes and 16 seconds stood for eight years, until beaten by Andy Wilkinson, arguably the only person capable of getting near it, by a microscopic margin of 58 seconds.

Once Alf decided to apply for reinstatement it immediately curtailed any further riding in independent or professional racing. To do so would have set back the application for another year. This meant no racing; nothing. Alf was caught in a limbo between amateur and professional status at the age of 22, unable to do either. There is some ambiguity as to a waiting period of five years, but in practice applications were made on a regular basis and it should have been resolved by a relatively swift transition back to the amateur ranks, hopefully within a year or two. It didn't work out like that. The divisions between amateur and professional status were entrenched, with independent status suffering from being neither one thing nor the other. The category was abandoned entirely in 1966, but even in the midst of Alf's suspension this didn't help. Previous independents were viewed with intense suspicion by those on the amateur side of things: a murky world where money changed hands, and bikes were fixed by paid mechanics, not by the honest rider on a spare blacksmith's anvil.

At the time, the divisions were closely guarded and rigidly applied. Those in charge of the amateur side of sport, essentially the RTTC, saw themselves as the guardians of a longstanding tradition and it became a matter of quasi-ideological purity. It is again worth remembering that Bidlake's codification of the sport's ethics and regulations was within relatively recent memory. Those governing the sport and enforcing the rules would have been time triallists in the 1930s. Anything that might taint the seriousness and the simplicity of amateur sport had to be resisted. There were myriad examples of transgressions – most ridiculously minor. People taped over trade names on shoes and shorts ("I had a pair of Clive Stuart shorts that, thanks to my Mum, said 'Live Art'," says one old tester), and the names of frame builders needed to be suitably obscured, hence the use of swirly script, and more interestingly, unusual frame design. Both the Hetchins curly seatstays and the Bates cantiflex forks came from a desire to make frames recognisable in the absence of other distinguishing features. A picture in *Cycling* of Doug Meekins winning the North Roads Hardriders in 1966 had the maker's name clearly visible: it led to a stern reprimand. Similarly, super-fast rider Lorna Hanlon was suspended from competition in the early 1960s for the unforgivable offence of allowing a photograph of herself to be taken whilst racing and published, which clearly showed the frame builder's name.

The individual was secondary to the principle. It was a debate that lurked beneath the surface throughout the 1960s, 70s and 80s, but was at its apotheosis in the early 1960s. Barbed comments and questions were raised in regard to equipment: being given a bike or supplied with a jersey was enough to challenge the amateur status of a rider. It's evident in the letters pages of *Cycling*, a jab and riposte of conflicting arguments: 'Disgusted of Addiscombe' complaining about the provision of a bicycle for a rider, arguing he is no longer an amateur and therefore must be expelled with immediate effect. Gentler voices pleaded for sanity. Within this context Alf Engers became a pariah to some, representing filthy lucre, a contaminating disease to be resisted and vaccinated against. His return to the ranks was resisted with absolute rigidity.

It wasn't just Alf: John Woodburn came up against a wall of intransigence when he applied to rejoin the amateur ranks. Each application to the BCF cost £25*, with no guarantee of success. Woodburn gave up; Alf stuck at it. Right up until 1968 Alf's applications were rejected. In retrospect, it was an act of calculated cruelty, devoid of compassion and empathy, where the individual in question was a threat to the values of amateur sport. Alf came to embody these anxieties. A straightforward return to riding in the events he loved would taint the events themselves. He must pay the price! Each year he met with the blank stare of officialdom.

It wasn't the last time Alf would fall foul of the committee's decision, taken behind closed doors and communicated without recourse. It is also possible to see in this a general antipathy towards the Barnet club riders, a team bold enough to beat the establishment

---

* More than £500 at today's values.

favourites, who resisted the frequent attempts to be squashed into line. They had the temerity to ride with style and challenge the way things were done. They laughed at things in a sport where laughing at things was no laughing matter.

With little else to do, Alf rekindled his love of serious carp fishing. Entry fees were stiff, but the prizes on offer were much bigger than anything in amateur or independent cycling.

"It was hardcore stuff. We'd go to Peterborough: the lake was linked to the power station, where they used warm run-off water in the course; they had this aquarium running off of the main river. You'd have all these nutters, like me, fishing in the snow because of the carp. The use of technology was beginning to take off: people would 'go full-time', pack in their jobs and make a living fishing for carp."

I found this difficult to believe. However, memories suddenly emerged of a trip I took to Devon to see my mum. She had parked her camper bus on a farm outside North Molton which had a fishing lake. We went for a walk around the lake. I was unprepared for the level of commitment from the fishermen: they had wheelie trolleys and alloy flight cases for their gear. The set-up on the bank looked like something out of GCHQ – an array of high-tensile rods in harness, tension meters reading for the slightest twitch, flurry or dip in surface tension. The struggle was real. I mentioned this to Alf.

"Yes, and it's changed even more. Back in the day the whole thing was evolving. Dave Moore wrote a book about it, and there is a story where it's early summer, June maybe, and he asks this other bloke how long he is going to be fishing for, thinking 'today, maybe tomorrow'. The bloke says, 'I can only stay till October.' People would be there so long they ended up with bushes growing up around them. The money crept in and it changed things, with the importation of foreign fish to the lakes. A chap broke the record for a carp recently, but it was an imported fish. It caused a stir; he got death threats: 'You claim that carp and you'll be sleeping with his pals by the end of the week'."

Alf was always looking for the big carp. "The biggest fish I caught back then – one of the ones you see in the photos – it was 19lb, and I caught it out at Dagnum." I listen intently with my untrained West-country ear. I assume Dagnum is a sleepy village somewhere in

Hertfordshire. I sense an image of Alf at peace within the tranquil countryside, removed from the chaos of the capital.

"Where sorry... Dagnum?"

"DAGNUM. I had an exchange ticket for the Dagnum Anglers' Club, used to head over that way."

"What, DAGNUM?"

"Yes, DAGNUM."

"Wait... DAGENHAM? Where the Ford plant was?"

"Yeah, that's right. DAGNUM. I used to love heading out to Naezing Meads in the Lee Valley. It's a feeling of escape. But then kit started disappearing, gangs appeared. It's teetering on the brink and I won't go there anymore. I head abroad. I loved night fishing, the tranquillity, getting away from it all. There are very few tranquil places left anymore. You're in the age of full-time everything. How the hell do you live?"

There is some truth in the idea that there is no time, but there is also a tension. By way of comparison, it takes me ages to write a book, much longer than I would like, and that's because I work at the same time. But then, I don't see work as a way of life, more as something that enables me to write, to do something on my own terms which isn't linked to work. It is a hard balance to strike and at times it has been impossible. It has been the writing that suffers, I have had to work. I wonder if, for Alf, pursuing cycling as a line of work, as an independent, meant he could no longer do it on his own terms. But, equally, that is a reductive argument: he clearly dreamt of success, of riding the big races and being a part of the peloton. But his commitment to work and his values meant that it was never likely to be viable. The push and pull factors in the end led to a tension that didn't dissipate.

It's certainly true that the reason he time trialled so much is that it can be done on a reduced training load: you can fit it around the other things you have to do. Work to live, not live to work. As to whether this is because he wanted it to be like that, or because that was the way life panned out, is harder to judge. What is clear is that for five long years, from the age of 22 to 27, Alf Engers was unable to ride competitively. It is an outcome that cannot be considered as anything other than vindictive and deeply unfair.

With his usual wistful equanimity, Alf sought to fill the void left by cycling in other ways. Aside from the carp, baking and family life, Alf turned to fashion and music. As you do.

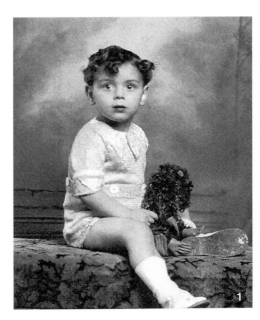

Circa 1943 with an indeterminate stuffed creature

'It was a rusty hand grenade. I was thrilled to find it.'

Both kneecaps intact

Cycle speedway

With Old Al at Herne Hill, 1959

Winning at Herne Hill, Good Friday 1959

First road race win by a tyre at Stapleford Tawney

The Champions' Dinner in 1960, with Woodburn and
Harvey receiving the trophy from Jacques Anquetil

The Skiffle Years

At the1969 Championship

*First '25' on his comeback,
now beardless...fatter*

The all chrome Shorter

13

*The Farnham course
in the early 1970s*

14

1975 Brentwood CC

Lesson 7

Length is most important, you want it to drape to your fingertips

Before cycling, Alf was always keen on music and clothes. It was a key part of his formative years, shaped in late 1950s London. In the run up to the end of rationing in 1954, tailors on Saville Row began to revisit the Edwardian suit for wealthy clients in the City. It had three clear effects: it reasserted the Saville Row guild and their sartorial expertise; it was an ostentatious display of luxury for the wearer; and it marked a break with the past, despite its origins. It was a new fashion and a clear demarcation from the austere postwar years. However, it was also class-based and, arguably, an attempt to reinforce the hidden barriers within British society, and re-establish prewar hierarchies as a reaction to the increased social mobility of the middle and working classes. The only problem with this ideal was that those pesky, working-class youths immediately co-opted the style, appropriating it and adapting it to their own ends. It was metropolitan at first; and Alf was one of many to create his own bootleg version of the Edwardian look.

"I was 16 and we were still in the era of the suits. Just after the war, teenagers didn't have an identity: if you were a teenager, a kid in the late 1940s or 50s, you aped your dad with sports jackets and grey flannels. It wasn't until the American influence that things changed, with the introduction of gabardine. People would wear a midnight blue gabardine suit with a cutaway collar on the jacket and knitted tie. This shifted into the Edwardian look, the Teddy boy, with a four button jacket and velvet collars.

"I went to the tailors with my dad, 'The Defiance', on the Caley Road. It was probably the only suit he ever bought me. I knew exactly what I wanted. It had to be handsewn, a corner like a ha'penny bit. It needed a drape hanging straight down. Length is most important; you want the jacket to drape down to your fingertips, and my father didn't want that. We had the measuring up, and then left the shop. I conveniently told him I had just 'forgot' something, went back in and told him to drape it, to get the length just right.

"Later, at another tailors I had a pair of trousers made and the tailor said, 'You seem like the kind of person who might be interested in this,' and he came out with this beautiful midnight-blue jacket with a velvet collar. He knew. Ten minutes later I'm strolling down the road. I've still got it now."

The American influence on British popular culture extended further, with the appropriation of music, initially with the trad jazz boom and then Skiffle, with Ken Colyer's column in *Melody Maker* becoming a compelling influence for the postwar generation. By early 1953 the fire was lit and Ken Colyer's Jazz Band began to shake up the moribund postwar world of crooning, and the easy-listening big band. A gig at Acton Town Hall early that year became an epiphany for a young Pete Townshend, a Londoner of similar age to Alf:

> I was used to the tidy music of my dad's era. It was messy. The band were messy, the audience were messy... they were drunk, they wore cheap rough duffel coats, some had wet themselves... I could see the end of my father's world – I was going to get this guitar and it was going to be bye-bye, old-timer, and that's exactly what happened.[13]

Colyer was an important figure in the skiffle boom. In 1954 Chris Barber took on leadership of the band when Colyer left, and they headed into the studio on 13 July, 1954, with Lonnie Donegan using up spare time to record a set of skiffle songs including 'Rock Island Line'. Despite a slow burn, within 18 months skiffle exploded in popularity. The combination of Teddy Boys, with their reputation for danger and unease, a reaction against the past aligned to the dynamic accessibility of skiffle with washboard and tea-chest, forged the first postwar youth subculture. Unsurprisingly, Alf was on board for the ride. It is as though Lindsay Anderson's contemporary manifesto for film was written for the North Londoner:

> Size is irrelevant. Perfection is not an aim. An attitude means a style. A style means an attitude.[14]

"Ken Mackintosh did the first record I really paid attention to: 'The Creep'. It was this strange dance which you did together. It was popular with the Teddy Boys, and it went from there. I was in a couple of skiffle groups: the Misfits, and the Skellingtons. It was a quintessentially British thing at the time. It hadn't come from elsewhere. It was our music. It was accessible: a tea-chest bass, guitar and three chords. Unfortunately most people didn't want to sing; everybody was shy. In the end I thought, 'Bugger this; I'm not shy.' We played these coffee bars, 'Chiquitos', opposite the 'Dominion'. You had to play for an hour or two hours, then pack up and leave, so they could clear up. We'd go to Lyons corner house, eat, then go back and start again, before finally catching the midnight tube home. We used to see the London Underground steam train, one of the last remaining ones which they used for the cleaners when the underground was otherwise closed. We played all around the West End; you got 30 bob. It was fun. All of a sudden you had this music which you could make in your bedroom. We hadn't heard of many of the songs at the time and they were easy to play.

"The chap who taught me how to play guitar was a long-distance lorry driver, Tommy McFadden, who used to bring people down from Glasgow. He brought Gus Mackenzie, who had a background in Country and Western, after living in Tennessee. Later on he got involved with George Martin who gave him the stage name 'Carl Denver'. A lot of the time he got drunk and didn't turn up for gigs. He was in the skiffle group. We did a mini-competition at the Finsbury Park Empire. One heat I sang, we got through; the one Gus did we didn't get through. Like most of the older halls, Finsbury Park has been knocked down; it's a block of flats. Gus didn't have a guitar so my mate, Terry Hicks, lent him a guitar. Terry was a window-cleaner and did the windows at Buckingham Palace. He got an MBE for that.

"Anyway, all of a sudden Gus buggered off with the guitar. We tracked him down to a house in Fulham where all the musos of the age lived, with the hot band then, *The Vipers*. 'Hello, is Gus there?' we asked. We just waited outside in a corner shop and lo and behold, two hours later, Gus comes out with the guitar. We said 'Er... yeah... the guitar, Gus.' It takes a worried man to sing a worried song. That certainly applied to Gus at that moment."

Judith hears us talking from the room next door. She hears the reminiscence, the stories of songs and their singing. "Whatever you do," she says, "don't ask him to bloody sing."

We talk about 'Green Corn', by the Avon Cities Skiffle Group, with Ray Bush on vocals; 'Alabammy Bound' by Lonnie Donegan; 'Steamline Train' by the Vipers; and Alf looks at me with mild bemusement.

"How do you know these songs?"

And I have to explain how I love Lonnie Donegan – the raw, belting music, pure kinetic energy, and the unmistakeable angular appearance and rhythmic forcefulness. All words which seem applicable to Alf in his chosen medium of bike riding at speed. And I explain how it was a bit of a gateway drug to a whole world of skiffle, and how I have a theory that time trialling is like skiffle, which is, in turn, like the Teddy boys and Grime music, insofar as they are things that are British and quirky, and esoteric and folk. I revisit the Dizzee Rascal Time Trial hypothesis and he gives me a funny look, as if he doesn't really share this view of the world. But I like to think he does, secretly.

Throughout the middle of the decade Alf had more time on his hands than he knew what to do with. He spent a lot of it on the riverbank, but he also took the opportunity to become a fully fledged participant in everything swinging London had to offer.

"I basically adopted a hippy lifestyle. I was even a member of the Pagan Federation, right up until about five years ago when I started seeing ads for Druid courses, and Goddess courses, courses on how to live and wondered what the hell they were talking about. All those hippies are probably working in banks now. It was a dream, a free-and-easy period which I loved. It was also the first time I got a fur coat, which became a bit of a trademark later. I bought it off a girl for fifteen pounds. I used to turn up to races in it, this big thick Afghan coat. That was the fashion then. There weren't a lot of cyclists turning up to bike races in fur coats. It wasn't mink, maybe it was musquash or something.

"When you got to the so-called psychedelic era, with The Beatles and the outrageous dress and hair, and drugs, that was a different era completely. Things are different again now. I made a mistake when going to the Pickwick Club dinner. I thought, 'I'm not going to wear a club tie.' I wore a bow tie, and you should have heard them: 'Does that turn round? Does it light up?' I come from an era where you put on your Sunday best and none of the shops were open. Of course, now all of the shops are open and it's very casual. It's not the same."

"The Teddy still suits him best," says Judith, from the next room.

Lesson 8

There is nothing more important
than a single second

After five years of pagan living, high fashion and carp, Alf had one last go at getting reinstated in 1968, hoping to start racing again in 1969. He managed to amass an array of doctor's certificates arguing that he was unsuited to the professional or independent ranks, for medical reasons.

> Due to significant trauma and damage to the right patella, in particular the articular cartilage and synovial membrane, but also the femur and joint capsule, it is not possible for Mr Engers to ride at the highest level. As a medical practitioner and clinical expert it seems that amateur sport is the only route open to him in order to pursue his chosen sport, in this case, cycling. Even so, with a significant proportion of the patella being missing and what remains being fragmented, it is unlikely he will experience further success, given the difficulties he has walking.

Essentially, the argument was that with his kneecap missing he could barely stand up. Confronted with extensive written medical evidence and several years of absence, they finally relented. At last, Alf was back on the bike at the age of 28, having missed most of his best years. There was no fanfare, no sense of the glorious return of a lost hero – Alf may have managed to attain the competition record in 1959, but he had never won a national title. The sport had moved on: many of the older riders had gone; new ones had come in.

The fastest of the new breed was Dave Dungworth, who had lowered the '25' record to 52-18 in August 1966. Dungworth was a compact, lightweight rider who had put everyone to the sword over the course of two astounding seasons. On Alf's return, Dungworth was heading in the opposite direction. However, he had similar difficulties managing the increased training load, and after two years retired from road racing altogether. There was to be no comeback, and the battle many would have liked to have seen – Dungworth v Engers – never happened. It provided a subtext to Alf's comeback, but even so, Alf was yesterday's man and no-one seemed especially bothered by his return to the sport. His first ride back was a humbling experience.

"I hadn't as much as ridden the bike in about five years, so I started to ride, around Christmas time. I went out for a long ride on New Year's Day and got to within five miles of home. I was totally exhausted and could go no further. I found a phone box and rang Old Al, who had to come out to get me. Training was very hard and I started to enter road races. The first six applications were turned down, apparently with the reason that my club didn't promote road races. After that I decided to enter time trials again."

Unsurprisingly, he came into the new season a little over race-weight. He took to the start line in March for his first open time trial since 1961, at the Viking Road Club promotion on the Southend Road. Alan Gayfer was complimentary and blunt in the same paragraph, and as lyrical as ever:

> Now beardless, fatter, at 12 stones self-confessedly two stones overweight, but with 2,600 'easy miles' in his legs, he has thrown the first banderilla* which will torment the bulls of short-distance time trials in 1968. Alf will never be able to represent his country as an amateur in the World or Olympic championships, but his class is evident, despite his thickness around the waist.

The themes resurface and are picked up again in Gayfer's last paragraph:

> Still young, he's turning to amateur racing again, his past expunged by a sympathetic committee. Always ambitious, always realistic, he remains so today. It will be interesting to see if he can maintain and improve on this form.[15]

It's difficult to gauge exactly what Gayfer means by 'sympathetic committee'. It seems somewhat at odds with the reality – a pedantic

---

* the small dart used by a toreador.

board safeguarding against the evils of 'tainted' riders by excluding any of those they felt had transgressed. It is acknowledged that the door to international selection had been slammed shut, but with no reflection, nor comment on the effect this might have had on Alf. In some ways, there was no ambiguity either; once you crossed the Rubicon there could be no turning back. It doesn't matter what we think about it now, from our ultra-professionalised world, where amateur status is at times marginalised as a quaint and strange affectation. It was the line in the sand.

Yet, for all cycling's apparent callousness, things were worse in other sports. The amateur rules governing rugby in Wales meant those who switched codes were banned for life and often ostracised from the local community. A five-year hiatus seems remarkably light when compared to the treatment meted out to working class Welsh players seeking better wages and prospects. Most headed to the northern heartlands, never to be seen again. Again, it's hard for us to comprehend the values and the cultural context behind the schism. Suffice to say that those who are upholding the amateur ideal see the influence of money, whether real or imagined, as an evil and corrupting force. In taking payment, money becomes the motivation, with sporting performance being the key to earning more. The fear is that it leads to a pernicious atmosphere of cynicism, gamesmanship and cheating, and it robs the genuine amateur of the chance of success. It is a binary and reductive debate: for the amateur, honour and glory; for the professional, only financial gain.

In his first event back Alf was the only rider inside the hour and won by over a minute. "It was a comparatively slow time and I received a lot of publicity, which didn't go down too well with the North London Mafia. All that hoopla for a 59 minute ride!"

Overnight, he had transformed from portly returnee to genuine threat to the status quo. *Cycling*'s headline summed up the impact it had on the time-trialling world: 'High Priest Alf Crashes Back'. He was wearing a 'fine fur coat and the familiar sunglasses, to look like the businessman, jazzman-about-town.' His hair was short, cropped, and he looked sharp with a set of dark and modish sunglasses. Alf's years in Carnaby Street had been well spent. He grinned at the camera, laughed at the madness of it all and enjoyed riding his bike.

It was also time to change clubs; this time he joined the Polytechnic CC, moving away from the Barnet for a practical reason. "They had this cult thing going on at Herne Hill. Certain clubs had their own lockers, and had preferential track time. As a member of the Barnet you were not welcome; they made you feel like that. The Polytechnic was an ideal partner for roadmen and track riders and, because I had a leaning towards the track, it meant I was more able to get on at Herne Hill." He was resplendent in a shiny Poly jersey with added stars and some very long socks. He remembers both for separate reasons. "I was a good looking bloke. I got the starry jersey from looking at 6-Day riders. The club didn't have stars on it. I did. When I was younger you had to have your socks long. When I came back I still had my socks long. Reg Barnett said, 'You look like a bloody au pair with them,' and that was that. They went straight in the bin."

He started riding, started winning, and almost immediately the letters began to wing their way into the press. Cue an agitated Mr Ken McDonald of E10, also, apparently, on first name terms with Mr Engers:

> I had the unfortunate experience of seeing Alf riding in front of me for about three miles. During that time he rode on the white line in the middle of the left hand carriageway, causing many motorists to brake and change lane to pass. Granted he was once competition record holder and won the event, but surely that does not entitle him to flagrantly misuse the public highway? Actions such as this could help to bring our sport to an early grave.[16]

From a purely mathematical point of view, it's hard to imagine how Mr McDonald managed to keep sight of Alf for three miles, considering the profound difference in speed and his failure to trouble the timekeepers. Nevertheless, the apocalyptic fear of an end to the sport is a recurrent theme which still rattles around today. 'Such actions endanger the sport we love,' and so on. It comes down to the thin end of a very thick wedge, where any hint of an infraction from

Alf would lead to punitive measures from the officials. However, with every letter that presented Alf as the enemy of the people, another followed up in his defence, this time from W. Martin of East Bergholt:

> Everyone knows that you have to ride way out from the kerb to gain maximum benefit from traffic: this is the art of time-testing on dual carriageways. Everyone does it. Last year I listened to an old veteran moaning about "these youngsters taking risks". I could not help laughing, for I had seen him a few minutes earlier, tucked in behind a petrol tanker doing quite 35mph. He was a local RTTC councillor! Good luck Alf. There is a lot more traffic on the road now than a few years ago, and I hope you get your competition record back.[17]

The increase in traffic referred to highlights one of the eternal contradictions of the sport: taking pace or drafting is illegal, and yet the fastest courses (and therefore fastest times) tend to benefit from high traffic counts. Lorries and cars come past and don't immediately disappear. There is a lift. Lots of cars coming past is a good thing, just as a tailwind is a good thing, and a gift hill (one which you descend but don't have to come back up) is an even better thing. But throughout the 1960s traffic counts were low and traffic speeds were lower, which made it more complicated and harder to have an honest ride. I'm not making excuses for taking pace, but I am saying that the pace of traffic made it harder not to take pace. Riding at 35mph or more behind Granny and Auntie Betty making their way to Southend-on-Sea for some cockles was a tough gig, something identified by Peter Underwood of the Veterans' Cycle Club:

> Alf would be averaging 30 mph in a situation where cars may not be doing that much more, at times less. The RTTC seemed to think that Alf should just crawl along the gutter going slowly so as not to be travelling at the same speed as the traffic. Being competitive, Alf wanted to keep at maximum speed and this would entail overtaking slower cars pottering down to the coast. On a dual carriageway it could entail using the centre of the road and overtaking between two lanes of cars.

His views are echoed by cycling historian Peter Whitfield: "Why did the RTTC permit races on traffic laden courses, then object when riders took advantage of the conditions?" The answer is that the pursuit of time is the *raison d'être* of the sport and what drives it forwards. It is a debate which continues in the present day, although with far fewer courses available, thus creating significant pressure on the remaining drag strips.

Alf's approach can be seen in an interview with Gayfer:

> I just ride for fun, but fun can be expensive in cycling, and if Alan here didn't take me round at his own expense, more or less sponsoring my travel in his own car, giving up a lot of his spare time to help me train, I'd never be able to do it.[18]

It's an honest appraisal of what needs to happen in order to race at the highest level, but it's also another element which inflamed the guardians of amateurism. His injudicious choice of the word 'sponsored' doubtless was another banderilla to an already inflamed *toro loco*.

At one point revered clubman Vic Gibbons, BBAR champion in 1953 and 1954 prior to Ray Booty's three wins, ran off a series of 'I Like Alf' stickers. These were to be affixed to the top tube of the bicycle, giving a clear indication where the rider stood in the battle between Alf and the authorities. You can spot one in a John Coulson picture special in *Cycling* in January 1979, drawing together images from across Alf's career. Some 43 years later, whilst researching this book at Allen Janes' house/cycling museum/transport ephemera archive, he dug one out of his box of time-trial trinkets. "People used to stick them on their bike. It told you everything you needed to know," he said, with a conspiratorial wink and an impish smile. Allen liked Alf.

By May, it was clear that Alf was literally making up for lost time and getting faster, lighter and sharper. He made the rounds of '25' courses all over the country; the "speed king put another gem of a win in his crown. Using huge gears smoothly on the wind-assisted flyer to the turn, Alf defied the buffeting, blustering breeze in what was certainly the worst part of the morning and finished with a spectacular sprint."[19]

On 16 May he won by a minute and a half, a crushing margin in unpleasant conditions. However, the following week Joe Mummery beat him by two minutes, leaving Alf distressed and anxious. An opportunity for revenge came a week later at Basildon. Alf had been fretting and making changes, narrowing the block down to five cogs, upping the inches to 116, installing a plastic headset and a brand new pair of Clement silks. He then proceeded to turn himself inside out, thrashing into the wind and getting out of the saddle. "Again, I didn't have any money. I had an old pair of shoes. They were odd shoes. When Al gave me the time check at the turn I got up, pulled me foot out of the clip and knocked the back wheel. I had to get a replacement. You can't imagine how somebody would do that, but that is what I did. I beat Joe Mummery and I remember he ripped his jersey off, like the hulk or something. It seemed funny at the time. Apart from that I don't know him that well; he was a part of the North London Mafia." Alf still somehow turned the tables by a minute, and rode through to a state of exhaustion. Wherever he went, people turned out to watch, even if it was before 8am on the scenic Northwich bypass on a weekend.

The stage was set for the ultimate comeback, with the '25' Championship scheduled for the first week of June. It took place south of Manchester, on the main road between Goostrey and Oakmere. It was a lovely new strip of glassy tarmac with an enormous roundabout intersecting with the M6. Tips for the title the week before were Joe Mummery, Trevor Morgan and Willi Moore, with the *cognoscenti* leaning against a fairytale return for Alf. The jury was still out.

Alf pushed a 116" gear, putting an absolute monster of a dinner plate on the front to get the combination needed. He was lighter, now just five pounds off his fighting weight, but remained convinced that until able to pedal with complete fluency he had to go for the bigger gears. It's an odd philosophy, but born of the ideal of suppleness. It was good enough for a tie with Joe Mummery, in 54-52, a single second down on the winner, the 22-year-old air-conditioning engineer, Ray Ward. Alf coped with the loss of a second; he was sanguine and accepted it as a good return, given his time spent away. However, it preoccupied him later, and still today. "It comes down to the business of a second; there is nothing more important than a single second; races were won and lost, comp records equalled and not taken." It was the tightest championship race in history with one second covering the top three.

Unlike Alf, Joe Mummery struggled with the acrid taste of defeat. A single second on its own is hard to swallow, but it was compounded by the knowledge that if things had gone according to plan, he would have been the champion. That made it altogether much harder. Mummery unshipped his chain at the turn and had to stop and realign the wheel. "I'm not one of those lads who wants to go to world championships; all I want is the Championship." Mummery never did make it to the top step of the podium, a poor return given his dedication, character and talent.

Alf, too, had again missed the top step of the podium, but even his enemies by now expected him to come back strongly the following year. He felt confident and relieved to be back and had one goal left to aim for in 1968: the competition record. He wanted it back. It wasn't until much later in the season that he had his opportunity and it involved a trek up the A1 to Catterick, on a flat course in the flood plain of the River Swale. Alf viewed the Catterick course as a good one. "It was fast. When I first went up nobody had ever been up there before. There was a prize offered by the local cycle shop for their association record. I duly got the association record."

Dungworth's mark of 52-28, set in 1966, was the standard to beat. John Burnham, also of the Poly, was the course record holder and knew the out-and-back well. The weather conditions were perfect – warm, with a gentle breeze helping on the return leg. If you're going to have any wind on a time trial, it's preferable to have it on the way back. It was a fast day, with 51 riders breaking the hour and club records falling 'like ripe fruit at harvest time', as *Cycling*'s report had it. It became a season of single seconds. Alf equalled Dungworth's competition, but didn't improve it, although by way of consolation the Poly did set a new 'team' record, with John Cornillie becoming the fastest-ever junior and John Burnham as the third counter.

Riding out the season, Alf continued to visit the track and took part in the National Team Pursuit which featured alongside 'Scunthorpe Family Day', with women's hockey in the centre, making it difficult to get across and onto the track. Alf was riding alongside Ian Allsopp, Alan Rochford and Sean Bannister. "At some point Ian Allsopp had managed to get on the track and he hit one of the hockey players walking off. I've just got back, got no form whatsoever. There's go-karts going 'neeeeaah-neeeeah' and a full hockey match and the smell of hot dogs drifting across and I'm feeling really sick, and then this happened. We rolled out and Allsop's bike broke pretty much in two. He went down. Allsop was on the front, leading, so Rochford went over him and I went over the top of the lot. We were carted off to hospital. Alan Rochford was lying there pretending to be unconscious and we were all taken to hospital in an ambulance with Alan lying flat out on a stretcher.

"It then got surreal. Our manager, Brian Maybanks of the Polytechnic, burst through the doors and said, 'If you don't get back to the track in twenty minutes they're giving it to the Birmingham.' Alan Rochford got up – there's nothing wrong with him, only a bit of concussion, been unconscious, smashed his head, that sort of thing. Old Al called him 'Bone' because he was so thin. He suffered from terrible nerves all the time. I've got blood trickling from either arm, both knees, real hero stuff, and we got back to the track just in time. With the last lap to go Birmingham lost a man. Then we lost a man, I'd gone off the back. Maybanks signalled to slow down, I somehow got back on and we won by about a tyre."

The following year, 1969, started in a similar vein (minus the violent crashes), with Alf winning races, frequently by battling his way through mechanicals and ill-fortune. He was lighter, closer to the form of old, and resolutely back in racing shape. His hair was longer, a proto-mod cut. He overcame the close-cropped and slightly scary-looking Ant Taylor on the Southend Road, despite an enforced stop for a chain derailment. Both men were two minutes up on the field, with Alf a marginal 9 seconds in front of Taylor.

By now the descriptions and epithets of Alf were becoming more outlandish, with the use of 'King' more common. A mythology began to build around the 'swarthy patissier', much of it sparked from the pen of *Cycling* editor Alan Gayfer, who was never short of an expressive phrase: 'the great Poly rider'; 'computer-like schedule'; 'behind him all was lost.' By some distance his best description involves a dramatic recasting of the cyclist as a Faustian devil: "Enter the villain, right... the Mephistophelean character who came menacingly from the wings was none other than the man who stops top 25-milers sleeping o' nights. His rivals must have tossed and turned the night before, several had joked that he wouldn't start if conditions weren't up to scratch, but it was obviously all so much whistling in the dark."[20]

There was something different about Alf, and Alan Gayfer's rich and imaginative writing contributed to a myth-making process. It's in the Henri Desgrange epic style and all the better for it. Alf's charisma, outspokeness, attention to detail, and above all else, his raw, physics-defying speed, made him a captivating figure and his exploits leap off the pages of the Comic.

He has lost none of this lustre over the years; if anything it has been enhanced by periods of silence where he seemed to disappear, an emptiness punctuated by lone voices wondering what happened to the hero of their youth, the one who took on the forces of authority, the dead hand of officialdom, and lost, and won, and lost, and then won. There is something intimidating about his sheer force of personality, his presence, and the look in his eye. He is difficult to read; he gives nothing away.

When we meet I feel nervous, pressured, anxious. I'm not sure why, it's a preternatural gift, a sense of strident otherness which is unnerving. Judith brings in a tray of bacon buns at one point. They look amazing, a glazed brioche thing. I'm a vegetarian, but after already being late and already feeling anxious I can't bring myself to tell Alf that I'm a vegetarian and therefore turn down the buns by telling him I'm not hungry, even though I'm bloody starving, and I ram my fist into my stomach to stop it grumbling. And he keeps trying to offer me food and I keep politely declining and feel like a total idiot. I e-mail Judith later to apologise and explain how the mythology got the better of me and stopped me from saying something really straightforward. On our third meeting we take a lunch break, and

Alf disappears to make sandwiches. After bacon bun-gate and outing myself as a vegetarian I feel like I'm on safe ground. Alf returns with salmon and cream cheese sandwiches. I have to refuse them. It takes all my courage and strength. He makes me cream cheese sandwiches instead, and the dogs are happy with the salmon. I hear them tearing the sandwiches apart in the kitchen, and feel a little bit safer, knowing their appetites have been sated. Alf suggests I read the 1957 Heinz nutrition guide in full.

By late May Alf was ready to assert his authority and finally claim the title many viewed as rightfully his. All it needed was a clear run, no mechanical misfortune. Easy. Except on the Wednesday he was wiped out with 'flu and then the start of the race itself was an utter disaster, complete with mechanical misfortune.

"I got started and pretty much fell off, all in one movement, because of a puncture. I had someone waiting there with a wheel, but he panicked, he couldn't get it in. You can imagine; it was a wheel we weren't expecting to use, and it was decent, but it had a tooth missing off the top sprocket. He tried to get it in and it took about three quarters of a minute. Finally, someone helped me, pushed me off. My minute-man was Peter Watson and he started like a kilo rider, trying to get up, but he didn't make it. I relaxed a bit after that, thinking that I couldn't win anyway. I always wanted to know how it happened because I can't believe it. I was off as number 90. It started about 50 yards off the road and I punctured in the first few yards. Is that likely? I mean sometimes it's stranger than fiction but I doubted it myself. I think somebody did something."

Within six miles he'd made up time on Willi Moore and Brian Hayes. The pace was extraordinary, and onlookers wondered if it was sustainable. The answer was simple: yes. Alf pulled out time all the way up and down the road, beating Brian Hayes by 40 seconds (not including the 45 seconds given away at the outset). He regained his composure after a trademark lunge for the line, and almost immediately began looking for his sunglasses. "Where's my shades, I've got to have my shades!" was the plea. Several of the top ten were tested for drugs, with Alf unable to produce a sample until he'd drunk several pints of Robinson's and stuck his hands in water.

Alf had finally achieved his aim, a 25-mile championship title, ten years after his first competition record. In doing so he was the oldest ever champion at 28. Even Gayfer was wary of breaking out the lyricism on this occasion:

> We are used to superlatives in describing this extraordinary rider's feats, so much so that I am conscious that readers in some parts of Britain wonder if this is not sheer favouritism for the Londoner. Let then the bare facts of his win stand as mute witnesses.[21]

Even with the superlatives, a dark cloud loomed over the achievement. Accusations of 'following cars' became a theme, as did the sense that somehow Alf was doing something that he shouldn't – riding in a manner that was in some way contradictory to some essential concept of the sport. The key accusations surrounded two things: the first was white-lining; and the second was taking pace. White-lining was almost freely admitted; it was a key part of the sport throughout the sparse and empty pre- and post-war early mornings, but it was on the wane as traffic density slowly crept up. The Higginsons would ride in a straight line to cut the bend. Dead turns were also the norm, lest we forget how things have changed. You didn't need a roundabout, just a chalk mark and a marshall in the middle of the A road.

Taking pace was harder to prove; hence the obsession with following cars. It typically involved one alleged trick: a car slows behind the rider, waits for the traffic to build and build, before passing at a steady and beneficial speed. Repeated use of this increases speed significantly. It's an accusation that surfaces today and often swirls around the miasma of internet discussion relating to almost any record ride. One thing is clear: the RTTC was out to target Alf and looking closely at the issue of paced riding. They found nothing. Officials used cars to follow the rider in races in order to be absolutely sure that no cars were following the rider in races.[22]

Lesson 9

You do what Peter Post says

With the championship win secured, a previous competition record and a successful comeback achieved, Alf had attained a degree of fulfilment through bike racing. However, his personal life was unsettled and his marriage was breaking down. It was compounded by a sense of regret at his failure to make it stick in Belgium, a frustration at not being able to see things through and pursue a career as a cyclist, rather than a baker. At the same time, it's doubtful whether Alf could have let himself pursue professional status when something ingrained deep in his psyche seems predisposed to live by a certain set of values. These are predicated on a desire to work and provide, and are not compatible with the uncertainties of the pursuit of success.

In May 1969 he gave a candid interview to Alan Gayfer in which the editor of the pre-eminent cycling magazine in the land managed to get to grips with the latent tension that seemed (and seems) to preoccupy and drive him. Gayfer captioned a picture of Alf in action as 'grim... a formidable competitor who can drive himself to blackout point... yet can be the most relaxed and *soigné* of companions afterwards.'*

He also continued to develop the myth of Alf as 'the King', loading the article with metaphorical reference to the 'King of the Southend Road', accompanied by 'his cortège', and the 'grand vizier Shorter'. Even in 1969 the aim for Alf was clearly telegraphed: to win the gold medal that awaited the first rider to break the fifty-minute barrier over 25 miles. It had been promised by *Cycling* as the ultimate accolade, a once-only prize for such a significant landmark.

At the end of 1969 Alf rode right through the entropic autumn months, favouring the end of season events as he had done previously. With a peak in form and crescendo of speed came unexpected but heartening news and an official validation of his talent and speed.

---

* *Soigné* - well-dressed; groomed. Another example of Gayfer's ability to find precisely the right word at the right time.

Finally, after the years in the wilderness and the Antelope CC fiasco nearly a decade earlier, Alf was selected by the BCF to ride the World Track Championships in Brno in the Czechoslovakia. He had been increasingly successful on the track, winning regularly at the Herne Hill and Paddington Friday evening meets, including the Southern Counties Cycling Union Young's Brewery meeting where he won both the 5,000 metre pursuit and the Roadmen's '25'. He didn't participate in the joyously named 'Saxon Lager Sprint', but won money and lots of beer for his other efforts on the night. He caught Martin Roach in the pursuit, and it was evident to all that he was one of the pre-eminent pursuiters in the country, dispatching testers, roadmen and specialist track riders without too much bother. He won the kilometre time trial in the Nationals earlier in the year, gaining a coveted striped jersey.

At this point, Alf considered himself a track rider as much as a time trialler, if not more so. Getting the nod for World Championship selection was the biggest step forward in his career, hurtling out of the domestic dual carriageways and onto the shiny surfaces of the international velodromes. Furthermore, he had managed it on a regime of night baking and short, savage training sessions. With barely a week to go before the event, an abrupt telegram was sent from the UCI to the BCF, informing them that former independents were barred from the competition. BCF responded in the harshest possible manner by withdrawing not just Alf, but the entire team, dashing Alf's hopes of a representative ride at the highest level. Writing later that year in *Cycling* he was more than a little aggrieved: "I'm bloody annoyed about the World Championships. My morale was at zero per cent when I heard. I thought, what can I do now? My world is collapsing around me." It is hard to escape the sense of a lingering conspiracy and ongoing battle against wider forces who didn't want him to ride anywhere.

A feeling of bitterness and crushing disappointment was accompanied by anger at those who had destroyed the opportunity to ride on the ultimate stage. It seemed unjust. Phil Liggett interviewed him for the Comic in August 1969 in the wake of the farrago. It emerged that it was Alan Shorter who had told him the news; it left Alf shattered and contemplating quitting – retirement is too gentle; he never wanted to ride again. It was compounded by the fact that if he wasn't going, it meant neither were the others. Nearly fifty years later and the regret is still palpable. "How could I face the team – Willi Moore, Billy Whiteside and Ron Keeble? I got home and had no intention of riding the next day; the bottom had just dropped out of my cycling world." It was his previous independent status, something that in turn had already cost him his best years, which also did for his peers.

Things went from bad to worse when that weekend Alf learned that the Rockingham CC had taken the team competition record previously held by Alf, Cornillie and Burnham. The mark held by Alf and the Poly was three minutes quicker than the previous record and they were entitled to feel it might be in their possession for a while. The Rockingham had other ideas. Furthermore, two riders had carded long 52 minute times in an event on the Saturday. Riders were inching ever closer. Alf's supremacy as the King of time trials was under threat, and his records were being eclipsed.

He had an entry for the Stockton Wheelers '25' on Teesside at the Catterick course, and thought long and hard about whether he wanted to race. In the end, John Cornillie was heading up with his family and offered a lift and accommodation; it seemed infinitely preferable to staying in London. The only minor issue was that Alf's race wheels had been sold – all of his equipment was loaned from Shorter; he owned nothing. "If it wasn't for Alan and people like the Cornillies I wouldn't have been able to race; I didn't have any money for petrol or equipment." At the last minute favours were called in and they made the trek up north.

It was a typically lovely early morning on Teesside; grey, grim and cold. The wind was up and rising, and the conditions dented the hopes of the early starters. Many, riding the course for the second time in a week, came in a minute down on their previous times. It was a slow day but it didn't seem to bother Alf. His memories of the event remain preserved in aspic, "It was a funny day. I'd heard that on certain days there's just more oxygen in the air, so I decided to go for the record, although the wind wasn't quite right. It was spitting with rain and there was a lot of traffic. I started number 60; I wanted to be that number because the last time I equalled the record after riding into a wind for the first half which dropped on the return. No one will ever believe me about that," he emphasised with a cackle.

Despite the wind, rain, overwhelming sense of disappointment and absence of traffic, Alf hacked 29 seconds off the existing mark with a 51-59. Yet again, it comes down to the business of a second, which allowed him to be the first to break the 52-minute barrier. The Catterick course had been kind again to Alf. "The bike shop had changed the prize; instead of a prize for just the association record, it was for the competition record as well. So I got both." In less than ideal conditions, this dismantling of the old mark posed a simple question: how much faster might Alf go if the weather was good? Alf wanted another competition record – no surprise there – but according to Liggett, it was the carp catch record he wanted, not the 25-mile.

"It's almost ten years to the day since I got the record last time, with 55-11. It was a lot better morning then. I'm hoping that if, in the Ferryhill Wheelers event later this month, it's a tailwind finish, then I might be able to go faster. Satisfied? No, not really. I aim to put the record where blokes can't get at it."

It seemed ominous, a clinical statement of intent: there was Alf, and there was everybody else, the blokes. Comparisons were made with the 52-minute times carded down South in better conditions, compared to Alf's windy adventure up North. Not for the first or the last time, the question was asked, 'What would Alf have done?'*

A month later Alf recorded the fastest amateur pursuit time of the year at Saffron Lane in Leicester, with 5–01, then lined up at the Skol Six the following week against many of riders who had taken part in the World's. Alf was down to ride a special pursuit match against Peter Post, the bronze medallist in Brno a week before. Alf had strength and form and wouldn't be a pushover, but these events often had arcane rules and a series of secret handshakes, especially for the guest pursuit races.

"I was racing four times a week. Fridays were the paydays, the Charrington 100 lap – it was a hard 25-mile track race. You didn't

---

* This question seems to be the standard retort to any record ride. Alex Dowsett does 44 minutes. Great. What would Alf have done? Wiggins does 17-58. That's great, but what would Alf have done? And so on.

want to be going out in between. I was a track man, that was it. I would have loved the opportunity to have ridden the pursuit champs from 1969 onwards, but even in 1968 they made it impossible through the scheduling. They would have the qualifier on Saturday at Leicester and you couldn't get from Leicester to Catterick and back."

In effect, the schedule meant that Alf was unable to ride both events, so had to choose between two championship races. It applied to anyone dipping a toe in both events, but there weren't many others who stood to win both. Whether it was a conscious decision by both authorities to prevent further success seems unlikely, and certainly is more clumsy than anything else. The BCF event was moved to try and allow a bigger window for the weather with the outdoor tracks affected by rain. Ultimately, whatever Alf has said about being a track man, he wasn't prepared to compromise his time trialling for the track, especially when he knew it led nowhere as a result of his 'independent' past.

"I had the fastest pursuit time in 1969, but what happened next because of the business with Peter Post is they even stopped me riding in the National Championship. Peter Post ruled the Sixes and told everybody what to do – you do what Peter Post says, that kind of thing.* You couldn't get near his bike because it probably had a bigger gear than everyone else. He even ran the kitchen. I remember Nigel Dean, one of the riders, going downstairs for dinner and he was given a ham salad and they all had steaks. He wasn't happy. Nigel jumped over the counter and then they gave him steak.

"Peter Post came round early on and spoke to me. He said, 'We keep it like this for the crowd.' Then Hugh Porter came round and he said, 'Don't take any notice of what Peter Post says; he'll start like a rocket. Make sure you do the same'."

Alf was wearing a silver polythene shirt, described by more than one spectator as being made of 'bacofoil'; it reflected the light along with his matching helmet, and the crowd erupted when he rode on to the track. It was a dazzling piece of showmanship and the mighty Peter Post was overshadowed by the baker from the Barnet. It

---

* Post won 65 of the 155 Sixes he rode, earning the nickname 'Emperor of the Sixes'.

promised to be an extra special 'race of stars'. Skol director Ari Van Vliet was scathing of Alf's chances when speaking to Jock Wadley of *International Cycle Sport* magazine: "It doesn't matter... Post will catch him in four or five laps," with experienced Six Day rider Gerard Koel also chiming in, predicting a similar outcome for 'your amateur': "He may be fast on the road but he doesn't know the track and it's very difficult. Peter will be too experienced."

"I followed Hugh Porter's advice and I went off really quick. I caught him and he threw an absolute fit. Getting beaten by a bloody amateur, albeit that this amateur had been a pro. I got a year's supply of Skol for that. Post was particularly annoyed by being caught. It was demeaning. He never got over it. If you imagine the delight at the Skol Six, the sheer delight of the British riders; he went bananas at Ron Webb the promoter, ranted at him. But you know, I thought it was funny. Everybody thought it was funny. Peter Post didn't think it was funny. Years later when he was Dutch team manager, my name came up in the pursuit, he said, 'Oh no; he's been a pro,' or whatever, and that was it. They scratched me again from the team, and that was the last time I rode any BCF national championships. It would have been by the by, except that there were others, and they all got to ride. But the others weren't in the same boat; they hadn't annoyed Peter Post. This bloke ruled everything. I knew it was him stitching me up. Alan Gayfer told me later; Post was always there to have a word about it."

It seemed as though Alf couldn't go anywhere without annoying someone. Just his very presence and approach jarred with the order and precision demanded by a traditional and at times intensely inward-looking sport. Alf's fur coat and big Jag went down like the proverbial cup of cold sick. As if being extrovert and flashy wasn't enough, he had to make it worse by riding really fast.

He had one last effort for the season, a return trip to Teesside and the Ferryhill Wheelers event at Catterick. He travelled again with John Cornillie, the two were close friends and clubmates. John Burnham travelled as the third counter for the Polytechnic, and the intent was clear; to regain the competition record, both for Engers and for the team, putting the Rockingham club back in their box.

The Catterick course had by now acquired a reputation as the fastest course in the country, which would make the journey worthwhile. It's the same now: the sport of time trialling involves the pursuit of seconds. Courses that are helpful in this quest are much more popular than all the others. Riders travel to Hull (or used to, until the course was kyboshed by the local constabulary) and Resolven in the Welsh Valleys in order to take advantage of a sensuous stretch of tarmac. Record rides happen on fast courses in fast conditions, unless you're Alex Dowsett, in which case it can happen almost anywhere, in any conditions. On hearing of Alf's return visit, the local bike shop opted not to offer any more prizes, either for the association or competition records.

Alf was working to a schedule, the methodical process by which he paced the event, honed through years of practice with Alan Shorter standing at the side of the road, an encyclopaedia of empirical knowledge; how and when to stamp on the pedals, when to back off and when to ride. Both Burnham and Pete Smith (Clifton CC) were on form and a sense of suspense draped down across the expectant crowd. Alf was off at 60, early in the field. His schedule was set for a 49-50, and up until mile 22 it was in the balance. He faded towards the finish, but still annihilated his previous record and stopped timekeeper Stan Curtis's clock at 51 minutes dead. The curse of a single second struck again; 59 seconds sliced from the previous mark, but a second outside the magical 50-minute bracket. Both Burnham and Smith were inside the old mark, but finished after Engers, meaning their names didn't go into the handbook. Burnham was crushed, even with the consolation of a team record. If they'd finished before Engers they would have counted as record holders, albeit for a period of around 19 minutes. Posterity would have been assured.

Alf didn't hide his disappointment when speaking to Tom Stevenson of *Cycling* after the event: "I had the rough end of the stick; conditions varied. When I started I think the private cars stopped for lunch, because it completely threw me out in my calculations. I was pleased at first, but not when two other 51s came in. One thing I know is that I haven't finished yet. Today was not a good day; it was the competition that produced the rides."

A couple of things stand out from his comments. The first of these is the role of traffic and passing vehicles in particular in setting a rapid time. The effect of traffic 'suck' is known and a busy day, on the edge of acceptable limits, means a quick day. It is clear that Alf was chasing quick times and making the most of the conditions and the ways to be quick. It's not a question of drafting, simply that a substantial number of passing cars will have a positive impact on average speed. As mentioned before, this can incur accusations of skulduggery: a carefully placed following car might hold back, create a queue, before passing and bringing a stream of traffic through to benefit the rider. The RTTC remained hyper-vigilant, borderline paranoid in relation to this practice. The second element in this quote is the acute eye on what other people are doing. It is not enough to smash the record; any sense that others might also be near enough or somehow capable of doing the same thus cheapens the feeling of success. Alf wanted to put it on the shelf, out of the reach of the grasping hands of 'lesser riders'. This is the key to the penultimate phrase – 'I haven't finished yet.' Ominously for his competitors, there was more in the tank, and also a motivation that had been undimmed by the knockbacks from the BCF and UCI. If anything, it had strengthened his resolve to prove people wrong, and to do it his way.

Alf attributes at least a part of his success that year to a shift in training regime. "It was when we started to go onto speed training rather than just riding." He was spending hours behind Shorter on a motorbike. It marks a more modern approach, away from miles in the legs and onto relentlessly hard efforts, interval sessions and recovery time. Alf name-checked Norman Sheil in an article in *Cycling* the following year (a much more positive reference than his 'pain in the arse' comment of a few years back), 'coaches who are progressive... prepared to adjust to new ideas... a revolution in fact.'[23] Much of his advice seems relentlessly pragmatic: order club jerseys early; have a checkup; wear the right kit; stay warm in winter. The rest gives an insight into Alf's single-mindedness: 'Buy a large diary and make a training schedule: time up, to bed, miles, pace... Follow this as if you would be consumed by the devil if you did not. Self-discipline is the key to any success. Extra preparation should start two weeks beforehand.... you want to be like a wild animal by the time of the race. There's no time for pleasant chat. Forget about everybody. You're the only one who counts, and it's a win you are after. Nobody remembers who was second in a year's time. Give yourself exercises in discipline, for instance; I won't have my morning cuppa, or the afternoon one.' It is a mantra of abstinence, remorseless focus, and a desire to win.

Throw in a spot of gamesmanship and you've got the Alf of legend: "Finally, a pair of dark glasses to preserve a cool appearance and to stop your opponents looking into your eyes and seeing how shattered you are. A word or two spoken while climbing any large hill, to the effect of 'What beautiful scenery we have up here' could make what could have been his day, your day." Or a word with Jim George whilst sitting on his shoulder in the National Junior Championships, 'You've got this Jim!'

Having broken the competition record twice in four weeks, there was an expectation that something sensational might happen. Things were set up beautifully for the following season on the fast courses. The 50-minute mark was agonisingly close, just the slow march of 60 seconds, ticking towards the 30mph barrier.

On August 30, in response to a heaving bag of mail relating directly to Engers, *Cycling* went all in for a letters page special, publishing missives from both sides of the fence, under the title "Who likes Engers?" The answers were typically divided.

You may be interested to know that in view of the new Engers editions of *CYCLING* several copies have now been cancelled.

Now a top rider, one whose performances are at present the best on record, admits quite cheerfully that he is issued with his equipment race by race by Sh... you know who... I hope, with many others, that we may soon dispense with the pro-am distinction.

I feel disgusted that I am involved in the same cycling world as Mr A. Engers. I agree that no-one can take the credit away from him for his ability, but do we have to read about his weird personal life and continual 'on the borrow'? Mr Engers should realise that if he wishes to be a champion then he must set an example, on and off the bike. What an example to the young and impressionable cyclists!

It is emblematic of the staunchly opposed camps: one sees Alf as the living, breathing embodiment of everything that is wrong with modern cycling (and with a 'weird personal life' to boot, something I suspect Alf would take as a compliment), the other holds him up as a charismatic breath of fresh air, here to take on the doubters and move the sport forwards. Criticisms included the idea that he was somehow undermining the amateur status of the sport because people gave him equipment to race with, thus creating an unfair advantage.

The whirl of opinion and armchair criticism began to weigh on Alf's shoulders. It seemed as though everything he did, every turn of the pedals, opened up a debate or a challenge to his integrity, his place in the sport and his personal strength. Even the simplest of things, a light-hearted diversion at the end of a challenging year, could somehow become a vortex of recrimination and difficulty. And so it proved, on Saturday 8 November, 1969.

After a hectic season, Alf began to relax into the winter miles, alleviated by a quick bit of fun for charity. He was invited to appear on a float at the Lord Mayor's show, along with John Cornillie. The two were sat astride static bikes and had swords to joust with. It was a mildly diverting day out. Clive Stuart Cycles were at the peak of their success, with shops in Solihull, Catford, Stoke-on-Trent, Welling, and a new one due to open in Bedminster, Bristol. Clive Stuart also invested in the Good Friday meeting at Herne Hill, a staple of the track racing calendar, and insisted on the music from Bonnie and Clyde being played. He even had a full page advert in *Cycling* with a masthead reading 'BONNIE & CLYDE RIDE AGAIN!!!' as late as 1970. The Bird brothers, Ken and Alec, worked for Clive Stuart, one as a frame builder, one as a manager. However, the Stuart brothers were known for their profligate outlay. The business went to the wall and the demise of Clive Stuart Cycles saw the emergence, like a Reynolds 531 phoenix from the ashes, of Ken and Alec Bird's business as frame builders. In true North London Cycling Mafia style, they subsequently had a violent falling out and took a shop each.

The float was organised by the London Polytechnic and it was bitterly cold. "When the float got to London Wall," said Alf, "we went and had a cup of tea. We put on Clive Stuart tops to keep warm, got back on the float, had on full face masks like the fencers wear. We crossed these foils and one of the chaps, maybe Ken Bird, took a photo which he later used in an advert in Jock Wadley's magazine, *International Cycle Sport,* something like 'Don't fight over the bikes, boys, there are plenty to go round!'."

The RTTC got wind of the Lord Mayor's activities through the advert. What seemed utterly benign, a charity float, suddenly became a terrifying threat to the fabric of the sport: two amateurs were shamelessly promoting a professional business and had to be made an example of. Once again, the RTTC lumbered into action and made plans to ban both Alf and Cornillie, regardless of public opinion or any wider semblance of common sense. It's hard to escape the feeling of a witch hunt. Unable to quite ascertain how or what precedent had been contravened, and how it should be punished, the London North DC sanctioned both riders for a breach of regulation 15(a), inventing an entirely new and spurious category, that of the 'non-amateur'. Even now it is hard to work out what 'non-amateur' means. Whatever it might mean, they were both banned for a year.

"Someone initially complained to the BCF who ignored it, but they then gave it to the RTTC. I had to go to the committee. It was like the last supper with all these blokes with logbooks and a long table. They decided I was a 'non-amateur'. I had a club official with me, and there were these reporters waiting. The Committee member just said, 'No comment'. I was suspended, but I could race in BCF events. What is a 'non-amateur'? I mean, what is it? You tell me."

Both riders appealed in May 1971 against their bans. For Cornillie, it was more than just lost time. As Engers had proven, with a black mark against his name for 'non-amateur' status, it implied exclusion from all Olympic competition. The offence committed was wearing a tracksuit top, not wearing them in an advert. In essence, the RTTC were trying to determine what items of clothing could be worn in a rider's free time. Ted Kings, the RTTC head honcho, brought the complaint against the wishes of the BCF at the time. The BCF didn't recognise that an offence had been committed, nor did they recognise the category of 'non-amateur'. *Cycling* was staunch in their defence of the pair.

> Alf is a character, often foolhardy in his actions, but always the centre of attention where he rides, and he is not, repeat not, a professional. Alf has only been enabled to compete and to support a family because men like Alan Shorter, and now Ken Bird, have supplied him with equipment and transport... Men like Alf, whilst not paragons of virtue, are nevertheless essential to cycle sport. Cornillie is totally blameless... If the RTTC want to get tough, then let them give fair warning first, and we will all discard our local dealers' bonk-bags and tape over the maker's name on our bicycles.

There are some telling phrases; it's a measured response, even in its overt support for Alf. He is described as 'foolhardy', a known court jester with an impulsive and reckless streak. It is a deliberate choice of word; it isn't sinister or premeditated – it is impulsive. He isn't a paragon of virtue – that is reserved for the committee members. But then who really is a paragon of virtue? It wasn't Woodburn. It can't have been John Patston who was also banned. It can't have been Phil Griffiths, who was banned. The list goes on. Alf and the others were 'essential' to the sport, and I suspect it was this very fact that rankled so much.

The wider suspicion amongst the press and a significant number of cyclists was that this was a clear strategy with one outcome in mind, the exclusion of Alf Engers from the sport. The BCF wouldn't touch it with a bargepole, but it didn't stop Ted Kings and the RTTC committee. Any problems for the young John Cornillie, like the soul-destroying prospect of never being eligible for Olympic selection, were to be chalked up as collateral damage in pursuit of a greater good.* It was a problem that afflicted many others at the time, but few

---

* I once heard this described as the 'kill one, scare a thousand' approach. It is an utterly stupid, patronising and baseless strategy.

suffered to the same extent, and none had the same profile. Comments about the London North and the East at this time are damning: they were variously described as '...reputed freemasons... they seemed completely unlike cyclists, more like a division of the disciplinary ruling classes', and the more recent caustic recollection, 'the RTTC made the Taliban Militia look like Club 18-30 holiday reps.'

On appeal, Cornillie's appeal fee was refunded and his ban reduced, whereas Alf's appeal was deemed 'frivolous', despite it being the same 'offence'. "I couldn't understand it. It was the same argument prepared by the same barrister. To my mind the thing that runs through this is it's all a bit of a joke. It's just, 'let's get rid of this bloody bloke'."

The suspension gave Alf time to reflect and to process the events of the past twelve months, both the successes, but also the struggles and the opprobrium. It was his most successful season, yet it ended with Alf unwilling to ride again and angry at the public perception of his efforts and the pressure that came with every ride. When he didn't break a competition record people were disappointed; they expected more, regardless of the conditions. They wanted records every time he rode a bike, superlative feats to match the myth; they had to settle for a win and it wasn't enough for the crowds at the race or at home, following it intently in the pages of the Comic. Even when he did break a competition record, people seemed disappointed. Ranged against his approach and fanatical desire were the incomprehensible forces of authority. It's something touched upon by Peter Whitfield in his cogent history of time trialling, *Time, Speed and Truth*.

Engers had a fiercely independent, almost anarchic streak in his make-up, and he felt at times that the outside world, and in particular the time-trialling establishment, was determined to thwart him, to show him that they held the power, and that he must conform or get out of the sport. Whether these feelings were just that, tensions that existed purely in his mind, or whether he was the victim of persecution, is the big question. When we think of all the dedicated riders and races that they took part in we have to wonder why Engers was the only one to find himself at loggerheads with the sport's governing body in this way.

Whitfield tiptoes around the tensions carefully. Alf wasn't the only one to react, but he was one of the first and certainly the biggest. He wasn't prepared to accept the status quo. He wasn't prepared to roll over and accept the challenge to the individual and the threat of sanction. He's the prodigiously gifted pupil who keeps winding up the teachers, and refuses to be cowed by their shouting and endless detentions. He is Robin Friday, that wide-eyed and anarchic 70s footballer, crossed with Jacques Anquetil. His rebellious streak, reckless and hedonistic enjoyment of a gravely serious sport was provocative to key people within the RTTC. It invited anger and delight in equal measure.

The cloistered, furtive world of time trialling was unprepared for the cultural and physical challenges this posed. After years of defending itself, asserting its right to existence through clandestine actions and strict rules and governance, the sheer force of anarchy represented by Alf was a threat to almost everything held dear. However, for others his presence was a pulsing current of electricity, a galvanising force which animated the disconnected body parts and created something new, if a bit scary and overwhelmingly strong. The sport was being changed forcibly and irrevocably – from a parochial concern, reported in lengthy text and similes with endless lists of results – to a glorious photomontage of cheeky grins, gurns, and dandyism demanding of double and triple page spreads. There isn't a modern example, although Peter Sagan comes close, accused of boorishness and being a breath of fresh air in the same sentence. When someone breaks the mould, you can't then go and put it back together.

The RTTC didn't know how to react and the districts, specifically the London East, responded in sharp and vindictive ways. They got it wrong. All they did was feed the mythology and add fuel to the fire – both of Alf's indignation, and the wider sense that the sport was changing. Unable to force him off the road via delayed reinstatement, they opted for a harebrained approach which invited widespread ridicule and open disbelief. With such actions, any hope to win the war, even if they lost the battle, were futile. *Cycling* declared that 'Engers has been sanctioned because his existence is seen as a threat to amateurism. If this is so, then we must demand that the RTTC arraign others on similar charges... Rules are made to be applied and obeyed, but they must be applied consistently and not used as a weapon to batter those who challenge them.'

The emotive language, the semantics of 'conviction' and 'arrests' used in the *Cycling* editorial, indicate clearly the voice of the people. At that moment *Cycling* was the voice of time trialling and cycle sport, with Alf a regular cover star. It all points to a biblical committee unable to adjust and cope with change as the sport lurched into a modern and golden age. The grand narrative of a prelapsarian amateurism and the Divine Right of (Ted) Kings no longer held.

Despite his intention to walk away forever, the year apart seemed only to foment the desire to return and prove people wrong. After serving his suspension, Alf appealed to regain his amateur (as opposed to 'non-amateur') status, and opted to return in 1971. Even the date of reinstatement seemed a calculated snub from the Committee, "It was on the day of the entries closing for the National '25', so I express-posted my form to the event organiser. He sent it straight to the National Committee and he sent a note back to me at the same time."

Dear Mr Engers,

I have sent your entry to the National Committee. You have entered this National Championship 25 event in error. You have no business to do so. I have returned your entry and cheque accordingly.

Yours sincerely, D.H Terry.

Further national titles would have to wait.

Lesson 10

You need concentration, confidence and physical ability, in that order

In Alf's enforced absence, Derek Cottington had emerged as the man to beat. He had taken a leaf out of the elder statesman's book. Cottington was young, fast, and not afraid of saying how it was. He walked the line between confidence and arrogance, but backed up his straight talking with a series of staggering rides. 'Cotters' was seen as symptomatic of the new breed, riding 40 miles to work and back each day – a suburban schlep from Worpledon to Catford – averaging between 20 and 25 miles per hour. Tuesdays and Thursdays would see another 20-mile blast with the Charlotteville riders, whilst Monday included running across Worpledon Common, "the best way of developing my lungs."

Cottington won the title in 1971, a year after coming third behind Randy Allsopp. He had built his form on a frightening 25,000 miles per year. By 1972, Cottington was determined to bring the title back to Guildford and the Charlotteville CC and to beat Alf in the process.

During his golden year, 1971, he also achieved the fastest '25' recorded time ever, a 50-47 at the Oldbury and District event. It ended a drought on competition records: none had been set for some time and it was an unusually fallow year at all distances. Bernard Thompson's report in the Comic was laden with excitement and Cottington made the cover – a glorious picture of the young rider in full flight, long hair sticking out of a backwards cap, brakes lightly drilled, fingers feathering the levers on the way to the turn. His position on the bike was aggressive: low with an arched back, elbows at right angles and knees coming right up to the chest. It was enough to clinch the Campagnolo Trophy* competition for a second successive year. And yet still Cottington was disappointed: "I'm not

---

* Campagnolo Trophy - a year-long competition; the best in a series of 25-mile time trials.

very happy really." He had set out to break the 50-minute barrier at the start of the season, and now it would have to "wait until next year, I suppose." It gave an indication of his potential, his desire to rearrange the record books, and to steal Alf's crown as the King of short-distance time trialling.

Roger Iddles, the organiser, had stacked the back end of the field with the quicker men, banking on a straight-out dogfight and equal conditions for the elite. Willi Moore, Dave Holliday, Phil Bayton and John Legge were amongst them, with Bayton, who would finish fifth in the 1972 Olympic Road Race, off one minute ahead. Iddles had even laid on float* conditions: smoke from industry in the flood plain formed a long line skywards, uninhibited by a breath of wind. Bayton hammered a 118" gear all the way along the A38, but it wasn't enough: "I rode the race of my life today but he caught me for a minute!" A hushed crowd was gobsmacked. Cottington was the first man under 51 minutes, something people only ever expected Alf to achieve. The King is dead! Long live the King! Even in losing by a minute, Bayton's time was good enough for fourth place on the all-time list.

However, the inquests soon began. Iddles' careful field placement for the event was seen as irregular and liable to create 'paced riding'. The suspicion that Cottington had been 'pulled' by the rapid Bayton was sufficient for the record to be annulled. Cottington was philosophical about it: "I'll just have to do it again." Looking back, some 45 years later, Cottington insisted that the placement "can't make you do something you're not capable of doing. I would have done the same sort of ride whether he was there or not."[24] This is a moot point for anyone who has ridden a time trial: yes, you need to be quick enough, but the mental and physical effect of having a rabbit to chase is important. Otherwise there wouldn't be a regulation to restrict it. His chasing of the record and unchecked self-confidence put up a few hackles, as he later recounted:

I used to go to Herne Hill on a Monday. Reg Harris was up there. I didn't ride – I just went in there on the way home to see

---

* A beautiful term which encapsulates the feeling of a day when somehow the weather is ideal and the bike and rider seem preternaturally fast. PBs and club records tumble on such days.

what was happening. I got chatting to somebody and even then we were talking about beating 50 minutes for the '25' when my best was only 55. Reg Harris and some other lads came over and he didn't seem to think that it was a reasonable thing to think that I could do that, because it was 10 per cent. So I asked him what sort of times he did, and he said, 'Well, on here you do about 11.2 for 200 metres.' To which I added that it's only the same as you going down to 10.2 – it's only a 10 per cent improvement. This was to Reg Harris, five-times world champion and me a little nipper, a mouthy little git! I can't remember what his reaction was but we didn't speak much after that.[25]

The following year the cognescenti were looking forward to the battle between Alf and Cotters, something they hadn't been able to see between Dungworth and Alf some years previously. Both riders were training hard; it was coming easily and both were chasing the elusive 49 minute mark. Cottington felt he had what it took to topple the King; Alf felt there was unfinished business. Neither counted on the sudden emergence of a young rider from Hemel Hempstead, Pete Wells, who promptly scalped Alf in an early season race. Alf found the experience utterly unnerving, but for different reasons. It wasn't the loss to Wells, more the reports of following cars, with one of them reported to be a member of the promoting club. What is clear is that the cars weren't anything to do with Alf, and yet the constant dripping tap of speculation stayed with him.

"It makes you want to give up time trialling completely. I have quite enough problems with officials who imagine I have cars sitting with me all the time, without adding stupid idiots who think there's something clever in trying to get me disqualified, perhaps for life," he told Alan Gayfer.[26] Later that same weekend, Alf – now riding for Luton Wheelers and living closer to Alan Shorter's shop – won the Pennine CC '25' with a course record and the fastest time of the season, a 52-29. Barry Chick appears for the first time in this story, coming fourth for the same club.

By the time the National Championship rolled around, Alf was ready, Cottington was itching to race, and Randy Allsopp keen to prove he could repeat his triumph of two years earlier. The race used the U18r, a slightly grippy length of tarmac between Bristol and Gloucester. It rolls up alongside the Severn estuary and undulates gently, but with enough bite to hurt the legs. Host club were the mighty Bristol South CC, (of which I admit to being a proud member) with John Legge, Jeff Fry and Allen Janes representing. Ernie Janes took on the organiser's duties. Ernie was a framebuilder for Thanet. The frames were based on aircraft design, with a cradled bottom bracket, very much in keeping with the aerospace tradition within the city. In fact, many of the Bristol South riders, including John Kempe, were aerospace engineers working at Filton in the north of the city. Most of the others worked for Wills Tobacco, a benefactor and early sponsor for the club which emerged from the Wills Factory in the 1890s as a part of the working class leisure movement.

Ernie Janes and the rest of the Bristol South had laid on perfect conditions. The Gloucester Road looked lovely in the sunshine. As a blue riband spectacle, it looked terrific. Ian Hallam and Randy Allsopp were just back from having ridden the Tour of Holland, finishing fifth and tenth respectively. Alf turned up early, an extensive mop of hair carefully backcombed, framing his angular and chiselled face. He sat on the tarmac, knees up and hands clasped, cotton track gloves on. A steely look, no-nonsense, race face on, a picture of serious concentration. Helpers darted around, with Alan Rochford preparing his new race weapon: 5-ounce tubulars on 24 spoke wheels, 57-tooth chainset and 13, 14 and 15 tooth sprockets on the back.

Alf listed the attributes needed for the race ahead: "concentration, confidence and physical fitness, in that order of importance". It's striking that fitness is last, as though the power of the mind in itself is sufficient to will the rider through the course and the race, transcending any physical limitations. Alf expected Cottington to be the main challenger and was nervous beforehand. He instructed Shorter to check the times against Cottington. In the run-up Alf had ridden two ten-mile time trials; a short 22 and a short 21 on the Barnet bypass, before picking up a cold and laying off for the rest of the week.

The Barnet bypass was Alf's favoured training ground. A contemporary from a North London club recounts seeing him in the afternoons: "The road went from the Barnet bypass toward St Alban's and back again. He would park his car at the Barnet end, ride a very fast 10, then drive home again. The only thing moving was his legs. It was a joy to watch."

Another clubman also comments on the experience of training with Alf: "On Tuesday and Thursday a group of us left the Cambridge roundabout to train around the loop, but the speed was so intense that only Barry Chick and Alan Rochford were able to swap turns. The rest of us would cling on for dear life. On Wednesdays he did a '10' at the Danson interchange. We once did a 4-up; after a mile I'd gone through twice, looked behind and it was only me left with Alf. I couldn't even see the others. I held on, and we did a very short 19 minutes. It was like riding behind a motorbike." The sheer unrelenting power of Alf is a common theme from those lucky, or unlucky enough to ride behind him. Typical is the experience recounted by Barrie Smith, Welsh hardman and Commonwealth Games track rider:

> I was on the Carmarthen outdoors track, which is a rather strange 'D' shape. It was the Welsh Championship 10-mile Scratch. I was in the string sandwiched between Pritchard and Alf with a lap and a bit to go. I jumped off John Pritchard's wheel with all I had and passed him absolutely flat out; nobody could have caught me let alone pass me. Then I heard the sound of a slow engine, more like a derny than a bike and Alf sailed past. By the line I was half a bike behind the fastest rider on our roads and on the most enormous gear I have ever seen outside of an hour record attempt. And Alf, he ended up with the biggest trophy and was there, later, to talk and laugh: a real great guy.

On the day of the Championship, Randy Allsopp was out early, riding to a 52-minute schedule. He was moving well on his way to the turn, before being struck by a puncture at 11 miles and then unshipping the chain. It was a crushing blow for the champion, who had tapered from a 27-hour week and was coming in hot. "I lost all heart. It sickened me," he reported to *Cycling*.[27] It was Alf who was quickest at the turn, somehow eking out 35 seconds on Tim Dobson and Pete Wells. Ever the optimist, before the race Cottington proclaimed, "I'm not fit. I haven't been training. I'm not going to win." He was right, and began haemorrhaging time as soon as he set out, going nowhere near the record pace he had shown the year previously, or on his last outing along the road where he set a course record. Initially Engers was measuring against Cottington: "I held a little back until I had my first time-check against Cottington, then I went flat out. I knew I was in the lead." Cottington was "one of those people who was always going to do it but when it come to the day they couldn't. Day before yeah, day after yeah."

It was no contest; Alf won by an inhuman two minutes and seven seconds, with former champion, Ray Ward, a distant second. Cottington never quite regained the heights of 1971; he curtailed his training to a mere 45 miles per day and struggled to shake off the effects of bronchitis. He had further days in the sun, but in many ways his story is one of unfulfilled potential. There is one clear parallel with Alf's experiences, when Cottington, Bob Porter, Jeff Marshall and Martyn Roach won the national team time trial, which was seen as the Olympic selection event for 1972. However, the BCF opted to double up the road team, with Bayton, Edwards and others riding both the road and time trial events. Except they only did the road race and didn't start the 4-up, whilst Cottington and the others stayed at home, resenting the missed opportunity of Olympic participation.

After all of the back and forth of the previous few years, the brutal nature of Alf's win laid down a new marker. It was thirteen years since he'd first set the competition record as a callow nineteen year old, and three years since his first title win. He wasn't an up-and-coming star, but neither was he an out-and-out legend. In a sense the accumulated mythology preceded him. Even *Cycling* admitted that Alf had to battle to get through "without a brush with authority", adding another uneasy variable into the most controlled of races.

At 32 years old he had a few years left. "Alf Engers is greater than ever, crushing the opposition by a never-equalled margin. They don't call him 'the King' for nothing." Any hopes the RTTC had that he might have been firmly caged and disheartened seemed to have been swept away by his uninhibited charisma, determination and speed.

II

16

*We want the finest drillium
available to humanity...*

16a

*...we want it here and
we want it now.*

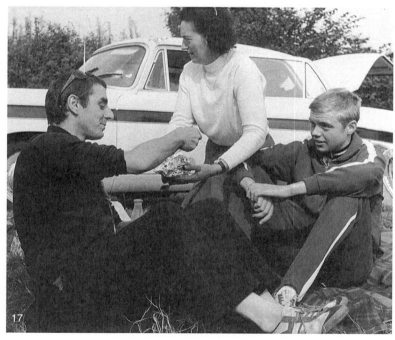

17

*With John Cornillie and Jean Burnham
at Catterick after taking the record*

Course record ride at the North Road Hardriders

A 19-pound carp at Dagenham

*Alf (and daughters) with Beryl Burton at the Champions'
Night in 1973. Both were rewriting the 25-mile record books.
"Beryl was head and shoulders above everybody else."*

Ready to go at the National '50' in 1976

Struggling home on Mick Jeggo's bike

Ted Kings and Alf

*It is clear where this rider stands in the battle
between Alf and the authorities.*

A busy trackside at the Skol Six

The Skol Six

27

"Concentration, confidence and physical ability"

Crowds lining the finish in the 1978 Championships

After the 1978 championship race

30

*The triathlon years,
with Zeus*

31

Talking about beigels

Alf presents Marcin Białoblocki with the 2018 trophy

Sheila Hardy, Chair of the CTT., with Alf at the 25 Championship in 2018. "She is everything now that the RTTC wasn't then."

Alf Engers
UNITY C.C. - HIRECONOMY
49–24
5-8-1978

Lesson 11

The line must be crossed
before the race is over

The following year, Alf was chasing his third title and a stab at time trialling immortality. Alan Shorter continued to mentor and support him and this extended to equipment, with bikes supplied by Old Al from any one of a number of frame builders in and around North London. Alf started out in the mid- to late-1950s on a succession of track and path frames, high-end for the time, but relatively straightforward compared to later race machines. For instance, he broke the record in 1959 on a path frame with chromed track ends and Nervex lugs. The bottom bracket was a cottered Chater-Lea and the GB stem was completed by the legal necessity of a bell. It was a standard clubman's machine, built for time trials. By the time of the Antelope 3-up in 1960, with John Harvey and Woodburn, nothing had changed. The initial comeback in 1969 saw some progression, with relatively tight clearances, narrow bars but no obvious concessions to either weight or airflow. Bars were fully taped, for instance. By early 1972, things began to shift more quickly and holes had begun to appear.

The desire to increase speed without a similar increase in effort has been the key to all cyclists' efforts over the years. The initial wave of development centred wholly on weight, and reducing it. Tube-sets began to diverge, with specialist lightweight tubing, often suffixed with SL for *super leggera* or super light, or higher numbers in later years, i.e. Reynolds 753. Pictures of the all-chrome Shorter machine in 1972 show tell-tale signs of countersunk holes and evidence of a nascent preoccupation by Alf and Old Al with drilling any and every available surface.

At the end of 1972 one single event did more than anything else to put drillium and lightness into the wider realm: the Merckx hour record in Mexico City. The frame was built to Merckx's specification by Ernesto Colnago using Columbus Special Tubing, a titanium stem made by Pino Morroni and a Regina Record chain. Colnago then set to work on the weight, drilling out the bars, seat post, chainstays and chain. Even the hubs had hollow axles and smaller track nuts. It resulted in a bike weighing 5.5kg, a staggeringly light machine for the era.

Within weeks garden sheds around the country echoed to the sound of pillar drills as components were subjected to the indignities of milling and drilling. Next to unobtanium, Drillium is the single quickest material know to man, as any fule kno. At high speed it acquires a harmonic resonance, becoming an ocarina of speed. The contagion of home-drilled components and frames led to some beautiful examples, some factory-made, and some pitted horror stories. The craze continued to spread, reaching its highpoint in the UK in 1973. Alf's all-chrome Shorter is a beautiful example, gleaming and whistling in the late summer sunlight, the idiosyncratic highpoint of the genre. At the National Championship in 1973 Alf was riding for Luton Wheelers, on account of the connection with Alan Shorter's shop.

Ken Plowman preserved the moment in a seminal side-on image which has come to symbolise peak-Drillium. Everything on the bike has been lightened. The chainring is lined with carefully concentric holes, the crank arm fluted. The rear mech has been drilled out along the arms of the cages – each hole a matter of millimetres wide, and the brake levers and hoods are a perforated curve with more absence than shape. The bars are drilled in three parallel lines from the top to the bar-end and around, the stem is also fluted, The seatpost is barely contained within the frame – no minimum insertion marks for Alf – and also drilled through and around, each circle countersunk with an engineer's precision. Clearances are tight, the gap between rear wheel and seat tube is barely discernible and the front forks are sharply angled. In full flight Alf's elbows are in line with the top tube and his nose above the stem, with limited vision up the road. It's the most compact position you'll ever see, and goes to indicate how much strength was required for the top riders to hold still for nearly an hour. There is no support, just core strength and determination. Alf's hands, in cotton track mitts, grip the taped ends and the edging of the dual carriageway slips by in a blur. There was nothing left to drill.

In 1973 both Ian Hallam, the superlative pursuiter, and Dave Holliday, the fastest engineer in all the West Country, were out to stop him in his tracks. Holliday had been there or thereabouts for a few years and Ian Hallam was one of the few riders Alf genuinely feared – although more on the track than the open road. By June of 1973 Hallam had amassed a formidable trophy cabinet; Olympic bronze, Commonwealth gold, BCF road race podium and numerous national titles on the track. He was a big chap and rode a tall Bob Jackson frame. In the championship Hallam was off at 51, unseeded and lodged in the middle of the field. He proceeded to reel in the riders ahead and immediately took his place at the top of the leader board by two and a half minutes. A murmur of appreciation rolled out from the HQ, along the verges and through the nervous riders warming up. Hallam had turned himself inside out, showing the crowd what they had come to see: the contents of his stomach. It took an age before he could hold a conversation and Hallam knew that whatever else was to follow, he had given it everything. A club official diligently cleaned up the sick, washing the coagulated rice pudding and Complan into the gutter.

Martin Roach was out of the running after a nasty crash in training. He had broken a crank and bruised his ribs, leaving a huge welt and discomfort with each pedal stroke. In contrast, Dave Holliday was hitting his straps. At 21 years old, he had plenty of time on Alf, 12 years to be precise. Three days prior, Holliday had managed 54 minutes, despite a puncture. Alf was recovering from measles and had at one point considered not riding. A short twenty-minute '10' in training convinced him otherwise.

Holliday was up and out after Hallam. He attacked the course and overcame the challenge of Hallam by 20 seconds, but finished fresh, rather than decorating the gutter with green bile. It left everything up to Alf.

Riding again in the colours of Luton Wheelers, Alf opted for a pursuit strategy, relying on his track skills and capacity for savage endurance riding. The time checks were unreliable, variously up at one point, then down. It was clear that he was in for a scrap and there would be no repeat of the previous year's procession. He paced it carefully on the quieter road, before rejoining the main road and steadily, remorselessly, winding up the 118" gear. His cadence seemed to increase with each pedal stroke until it became a blur of movement and colour, legs whirring in harmony with the bicycle and the miles slipping past in the hum of silk tubulars. The course finished with a four-mile drag of interminable suffering. It was the deciding strip of tarmac, a lactic-inducing purgatory. At the last moment he got out of the saddle and forced the bike up and over the line, coming in a few seconds shy of 54 minutes.

Pete Wells, the youngster who had unnerved Alf so spectacularly a year before, had less fun. His wheel collapsed underneath him and he dribbled home in last place. Alf took the title by 15 seconds: a clear win, but one he had to work for every yard of the way. Dave Holliday cemented his position as the nearly-man of time trialling with second place ahead of Ian Hallam. Alf was the oldest winner, again, at 33 years of age, and now had three titles to his name. The following year he would set out to become the first rider to win four in total. The old and the young pretenders were being shrugged off with a shake of the shoulders and a turn of the pedal.

In 1974 the championship moved to Wales. Alan Shorter drove Alf to the course at Usk, on a dual-carriageway circuit which is still used now. It's more or less the R25/7, the slower sibling to the absurdly quick 'ski slope' course at Resolven. Frank Dickens was there with John Arkwright. Dickens was one of the pre-eminent cartoonists of the time and had a long running strip in the *Evening Standard* entitled 'Bristow', in which he often referred to members of the Barnet. Alf Engers became a mythical figure, 'the firm's Busy Bee', an indefatigable worker in Bristow's office, 'one of the world's grafters', and rumoured to be capable of doing the work of ten men.

Dickens was a part of the cycling circuit, a bon viveur who loved the fellowship of the road, and Captain of Unity CC. He had headed to the championship to indulge in repartee and follow his friends. Alf remembered the occasion: "As Frank reversed out and around he heard this dull crunching sound. He'd driven straight over John Arkwright's wheels. Fair enough, he went up to him and said, 'Er.... John, I've just run over your wheels.' John was laughing, thought it was hilarious, another Frank Dickens ruse." He later found his wheels crunched into the asphalt where Dickens had left them.

"That was Frank. At the BAR dinner there are round tables, and one big, long table – like the last supper – for the assorted dignitaries. Frank drew an obscene cartoon. I said to the waiter, 'Here's a fiver, go and give it to the top table.' And it was passed along the table, and it got to Eileen Gray*. She saw it, pointed at me and made a gesture to me for us all to stop drinking. Frank revelled in all of it."

---

*Eileen Gray was BCF president and a lifelong champion of women's racing, including being responsible for ensuring that women's racing was a part of the Olympics from 1984 onwards.

It was a blustery day in Monmouthshire, one for the hard men. The quicks lined up to chip away at seconds, with John French, John Patston*, Alan Boden and Martyn Roach the strongest of the strong. Dave Holliday and Joe Mummery were off the pace, with Holliday suffering from an abscess in his jaw which required lancing the day before – hardly ideal preparation for the trophy event. Holliday held the course record, but knew he wouldn't be troubling it on the day of the championship. Alf had jumped ship again, leaving Luton Wheelers for the more elaborately named Archer Road Club – Cutty Sark.

In typical time trial mode, the early starters had the worst of the weather; drizzling sheets of rain and a vindictive headwind for the uphill drag back home conspiring to destroy any gains made on the race to the turn. The order of the day was 57s, with no-one looking remotely like breaking 55 minutes. A year older, and a year wiser, Alf was suffering from nerves: "I'm not going for the title again," he told *Cycling*'s reporter. "My nerves won't stand it. I had a pain in my gut this morning, a contraction is the only word for it. It gets harder every time."[28]

Somehow the level of stress and strain involved was increasing every time Alf lined up for the race. It became a constellation of anxiety: a fear of controversy and the over-reaching hand of officialdom; the desire to win and to win well; to set new records and see off the young pretenders; the fear of getting old and slowing down; the balance between working all the hours and riding as hard as possible. All these were just about kept in check by a forceful outward display of confidence and the infinite well of support from Alan Shorter. But it was tiring, and ultimately it conspired to create a sense of fatalism.

Alan Boden looked formidably strong, built like the proverbial brick shithouse, with tensile arms and cartoon legs, thin calves and enormous thighs, the Reynolds tubing looking gossamer thin by comparison. He bullied his way into the wind, gripping the ends, hunched down with his back in a perfect arc. A crowd lined the finishing stretch, a gentle

---

*Patston was later banned for submitting an incorrect entry form. The same fate befell John Woodburn. During their enforced absence in 1975 they took on a series of place-to-place records on a tandem which in turn incensed the RTTC and became an item at the AGM.

curve on the road just outside of Usk, willing on the tormented riders as they threw themselves into the gnashing teeth of the wind. A young John French maintained some *souplesse*, but Alan 'Bone' Rochford struggled and gasped for air, flapping like a fish on a line as he rode through the finish.

Alf waited in the car, sunglasses in place, track jacket on, door ajar, receiving counsel from Old Al who stood by the open window. When the time came, he got out, calmly shed the layers, put a glistening layer of olive oil onto the arms and legs and wheeled away for the warm-up.

He made the most of the tailwind to the turn, averaging 31mph out, with the huge gear spinning furiously, then took time out all the way back. On a day when no-one could get under 56 minutes, with Alan Boden fastest in 56-21, the crowd waited in hushed expectation for the time to be chalked up. A roar of astonished appreciation reverberated around the hall once it became clear he had managed the out-and-back a full minute and a half quicker, at 54-50. It was a sensational ride in any circumstances and he was empirically miles ahead of the competition. The tension eased and a smile – that winning, cheeky half-smile of Alf's – crept across his face. He was in another race, a different dimension of time and space altogether, such was the margin of victory. He sat silently signing autographs in Shorter's car, resplendent in a sharp shirt with asymmetric patterns, hair getting longer with each season, dandyish silk scarf neatly in place.

Later that year, *Cycling* ran another of their features on Alf's training regimes. The inset box featured the phrase 'Britain's most controversial cycling figure'. There was nothing controversial about the guidance offered, just advice to put in really big miles over the winter. Alf advocated 280 miles a week in January on broken roads and hills to 'build up reserves of strength'. Once the season started the focus shifted to 'speed training', half-minute intervals, sets of minute intervals, horrible patterns of nastiness that leave you feeling completely broken. It included some dietary guidance: 'don't eat anything strange, spicy foods are out, keep away from any meat in sauces, because you may have a job to see if the meat is all right. If you have to eat sandwiches, always eat cheese because that is the safest.'[29] It seems easy when you put it like that: 280 miles a week with strength and speed conditioning; a diet of cheese sandwiches; no meat sauce. I know now what I was doing wrong.

By 1975, the championship wins were becoming a matter of course; Alf was beyond any argument the fastest bike rider of his generation. He had changed clubs again, this time riding for the Woolwich Road Club. The constant changing always came with a reason, something practical or pragmatic, but also serves to emphasise that Alf didn't belong to any one club. He wasn't a part of a group or a defined fellowship. He was Alf. Even with the changes, the underhand tactics and the skulduggery pursued him. Lining up for a tilt at his fifth championship, the organiser had him off inexplicably at number 20, instead of the usual 120 or scratch position, both as fastest in the field and by right as the reigning champion, with the super fast Martyn Roach off a minute behind.

"The year before I probably hadn't ridden on the road very much. It blew a gale all bloody year. It could be like that. In 1961 I remember it raining for fourteen Sundays on the trot. Maybe that's why, but it seemed odd then and odd now." It's hard to see it as anything else other than an attempt to bring him down a peg or two. It also opens up the spectre of unfair conditions, with the later starters typically the ones to get warmer and therefore faster weather. It didn't matter to Alf. The incomparable Dennis Donovan, writing in the Comic, took up the mantle of hyperbole from Gayfer, to fantastic effect: "Who was it dared to suggest that Alf Engers, the 'King' of short-distance time trialling, is not the force he used to be? And who was it had the temerity to put him off at number 20 on the card, instead of 120 as defending champion? Bow down you mere mortals and do penance, for the 'King' lives on."[30]

The A1 was as suitable a bit of road as anywhere for the pursuit of time and truth. Wide, fast, slightly scary and not very pretty. Alf had rolled through a block of eight weeks training and was looking strong, a finely sculpted mass of sinew and muscle. The pesky Pete Wells was again the biggest worry, with Martyn Roach and Eddie Adkins the outliers. The startsheet had given Alf a "dozen nervous breakdowns", but he reached a position of equanimity, eventually. "I told myself during the week that all I had to beat was myself." His self-confidence and inner reserve was strong; he felt unchallenged and knew that in overcoming his demons and his anxiety, he would overcome the opposition. The bike was primed and ready, and utterly space-age. "I used 5oz tyres (141g) and with the bike all titanium I reckon it must have been worth about £400. The wheels were 24 spoke, small flanged hubs. I'd gone off drilling and reckoned I'd got a real bike now."

Alf turned 35 on the day and with each championship title stretched the definition of how long you could go on winning. With four titles already in the bag, he added a fifth in typically imperious fashion. Having rewritten the rules of short distance time trialling, there was one thing left unsaid. "I don't know where I go from here, or how long I can go on. You tell me. I'm still looking for the fast one on the right course on the right day. I'm in a good set-up now and I'm well pleased. I even took my earring off today to go faster. Everything went right for me today."

Others were left bemoaning what might have been, especially Eddie Adkins: "It was really hard. I don't suppose any of you saw the hailstones?" The race report underlined the warmth of the reception afforded to all the riders, but particularly Alf: "In the end it was Alf mounting the podium to thunderous applause."[31] He was a folk hero and an inspiration, and by and large unbeatable, despite everything being thrown at him. Everyone wanted him to break the record, again and again, and more importantly, to nudge it under 50 minutes. Despite protestations or the evidence of young pretenders, Alf seemed the only one capable of achieving such a milestone.

By the end of August he had bagged the '30' record, carving two and half minutes from Dave Dungworth's last remaining competition record. It used much of the same road as his '25' competition record ride in 1959, and Alf described it as a 'trip down memory lane'. It wasn't a good day, and most of the people watching thought the record would be safe. Alf opted for a 118" top gear and used it to brutal effect into the wind, before making the most of the tailwind for the last nine miles. The absence of traffic – it was an unusually quiet day – was commented on by watchers and marshals, as though somehow they seemed unwilling to accept that brutal hammerings of super-quick records could be achieved without the kindly influence of passing vehicles. The second place rider, Tony Gibbens, was eight minutes behind. In time trialling terms it is a very long time indeed. Alf's average speed was 29mph. Gibbens managed 25mph.

Increasingly, there was nothing left to prove; no-one had won more championships than Alf. No-one had ridden faster than Alf. And yet, he kept coming back to his earlier mantra: he "wanted to put the record where other blokes couldn't get it."

Lesson 12

If they want to, they can get anyone

After a time, the awarding of the '25' Championship became something of a processional affair. Alf rode through winter, did his blocks of training; some new riders and some old ones hit their form at various stages, only for Alf to win by varying degrees, and with varying degrees of emotion in the reckoning. There were few things left to achieve, apart from the elusive sub-50 minute ride record, and a possible sea-change in public opinion, with the naysayers converted, officials on board and everyone living and riding happily ever after. The record seemed eminently attainable in comparison.

For Alan Shorter, running a business and living life got in the way of mentoring and he withdrew for a couple of years. Through the middle of a golden run of championship wins Alf had to look elsewhere for support. Luckily, brothers Ken and Alec Bird were on hand and supported him with equipment, and particularly frames. Looking back, Alf professes an undying affection for the various Bird machines. They sit between the Shorter chrome goddess and the later Speed Machine, with a blurred overlap into titanium and the crazy world of bike exports which followed with the Intercycle brand. The pale blue Bird bikes signify both the furthest point of drillium and the initial move towards aerodynamics.

The story of Ken and Alec Bird is a lively narrative. It's a complicated tale of sibling rivalry and violent disagreement. The Bird brothers started out as framebuilders and shop managers for Clive Stuart Cycles, until the rapid dissolution of the Stuart Empire meant they became owners and managers in their own right. Up until that point, they were ostensibly a team, but the separation became fraught, with an underlying threat of violence hanging in the air as their disagreements escalated into full-blown Old Testament sibling warfare.

Essentially, they ended up opening a shop each. However, leading up to the split things became untenable, with all the hostility and pain of a divorce, chiefly surrounding the division of the old Clive

Stuart stock. Fights and arguments frightened the customers, who were convinced at one point that Ken was going to kill Alec, but with Alec being the bigger sibling, it came to nothing. Alf recalls visiting the Ken Bird shop and using the toilet, only to see an Alec Bird logo at the bottom, allegedly so everyone could piss on Alec several times a day.

Alec headed across London to the South East suburban corner, taking over the Clive Stuart shop in Welling, which had previously been occupied by Holmes (of Welling), a respected framebuilder. It attracted a string of high-profile riders, including Sid Barras, Hugh Porter, Reg Smith and other members of the Mercian Bantel team. Alec used to build and rebuild wheels. Jan LeGrand, 6-Day mechanic to Peter Post and others, would also pop in when around for the Skol-Six. It was a London hub. It also became a popular shop with a host of domestic testers, including Alf and also Joe Mummery. Ken's shop was at Green Street Green, a strangely named village near Orpington. Eventually, Alec gave up the shop to concentrate on framebuilding, whilst Ken closed his in the mid 1990s.

The Bird frame was fairly traditional to look at, but this belied the craftsmanship and attention to detail. Many of the components were drilled, typically the seatpost, and the clearances had come in further, with the white strip tyres nestling within half a millimetre of the down tube. Many of the ends were left open: for instance, the rear was a semi-vertical dropout, drilled and filed and left open to the elements. Brake blocks were filed down behind the bolts and the chainring was a filigreed snowflake, of similar strength and weight. On later variants the cables ran through the bars and into the bottom of the brake lever. Even the saddle clip was 'woodwormed' or drilled through. 'Alec milled it out, etched the headset and put in a huge amount of work on all the components. Before we took that out the door we were made to sign a disclaimer. When they weren't fighting they were a good team. Alec was a bloody good mechanic, having worked at the Tour, and Ken was a brilliant framebuilder.'

Early season events tend to consist of irregular distances, over very lumpy and grippy roads. They attract roadmen and testers, out to burnish their form, move from training into racing mode and wear a number for the first time. They are unequivocally hard, hence the widely-used term 'hardriders', and some particularly sadistic organisers even now seek out ridiculously hilly courses in order to reduce average speeds to bun-run pace, and reduce riders to tears. I put myself and Mike Hallgarth of the Anfield in that bracket, having been partly responsible for a 28-mile course in the Cotswolds which featured 1,000 metres of climbing. In essence, it linked together five evil and long hill climbs, via five brutal and treacherous descents. No-one thanked us for it, for some reason. Even Rob Pears, evergreen veteran and fan of the 'sporting' courses, refused to ride it. Whispers of 'assassins' rang out halfway up Stouts Hill. Sporting courses also form a key part of the season-long CTT 'classic series', with two distinct and prestigious mountain time trials, one at Buxton and the other at Ankerdene. For many riders these days, this sort of irregular event has become the antidote to flat-track testing, and a refreshing change from the overly-technological sport that time trialling has become. Yaw factor and slipperiness matter much less on a 1-in-4 ascent. The flat-track bullies tend to stay at home.

The North Road Hardrider is the classic curtain raiser and the most prestigious of the horrible races. The sinuous roads and rolling terrain, often combined with winter frost, ice and inclement weather, make it a true test. In February 1976, Alf opted to try his luck, if only to redefine some people's perceptions of him as one of the flatlanders or king of the big gears. He renewed his acquaintance with Ian Hallam after their tussles in previous '25' championships and on the track. It was an event Alf always wanted to win: it brought prestige and recognition, but came without the attendant pressures of the dual carriageway. Time was important, but technique, power and bike handling more so. Alf wanted to put right some of the whispering from the North London Mafia; the misguided suspicion that he couldn't ride anything else apart from a wide open space. He visited the course three times in the run up to the race, hurtling through high-sided roads and getting to grips with the rough surface of Bucks Alley, less than a mile of gravelly, pitted tarmac near Little Berkhampstead. "On the last practice ride I charged through as fast as I could." In conversation with Dennis Donovan in *Cycling*, he went on to hint at targets for the year ahead: "If I can pick the right day and get a 1-41 for the '50' then I wouldn't mind having a go at the BBAR, but I'm still searching for the magic day to get the '25' record."

Alf hurtled around, taking the existing record apart with nerveless rapidity, slicing 34 seconds from Bob Cary's mark. "I've had a lot of criticism from London riders who think I'm just a big-gear man and can't do anything but time trial, so this makes up for it." The time was recorded by Ted Kings, who happened to be the National Secretary of the RTTC from 1966 to 1976 and thus very much one of the blazers. There was no hint of controversy, although the event can't have been without a degree of tension; Alf and many others placed Ted Kings up there alongside Doug Brunwin, secretary of London East, as the two keepers of the pedantic flame of officialdom, the victimisers-in-chief.

"It was a persecution, definitely. It went on and on, it was tedious to the point of madness. At some stage at a BBAR concert, somebody or other – probably one of my mates – jumped on this trolley being pushed by a waiter with two hundred glasses, and they went all over the floor. And Ted Kings was making discreet enquiries: 'Was it Alf?'"

Alf still harbours strong feelings towards Ted Kings and Doug Brunwin, even now. It becomes evident when we are flicking through photos, putting names to faces and adding context. I scroll through to the next image and it's Ted. Alf is electrified; a current courses through. "THAT'S 'IM! THAT'S BLOODY TED KINGS!" he spits out savagely. "Blimey. I remember at the end of the BAR concert they had this hokey cokey thing where everybody formed a circle and him and his wife would dance round in the middle, with everyone round the outside, then moving in, you know, in waves. I was always trying to get in there and kick the bastard."

Brunwin also attracted his share of criticism and became the bogeyman to Alf and Alan Shorter. An apocryphal tale from Shorter did the rounds of the Unity members in later years: "Old Al was driving his lorry one night on a main Essex road when he saw in front of him on the pitch-black road, in a black top and with a very dim rear light, one particularly 'anti-Alf' official. The official can't be named here so we'll just call him DB. Alan and his fellow passenger briefly discussed the possibility of 'accidentally' putting an end to Alf's problem but conscience eventually got the better of them."

It's a fine line here, and I'm not about to shovel it on and depict either as the antichrist, when they were key members of an amateur sport, giving freely of their time to ensure that races were organised in line with rules and regulations. That is beyond reproach; however their manners and methods came in for criticism from riders on more than one occasion and a common theme emerged from those in the line of sight of Brunwin's beady eye.

Alf, of course, was one of those. But there were others: "It was certainly my experience that - decades ago - some district officials could be very 'authoritarian' and impose their will to sometimes stretch beyond the boundaries of the written rules. Doug Brunwin ruled London East with a rod of iron, and his presence at an event struck fear into many a rider and event sec. 'Watch out – Brunwin's about' was the cry."

By other accounts, he was the gentlest of characters. Brunwin was an engraver by trade and a supportive friend to many. Nevertheless, he seemed transformed by the experience of officialdom and the need to uphold not only a set of values and rules, but also conventions. In many ways, whilst Alf rode within the rules, it was the flouting of convention and cultural challenge that cost him. His riding wasn't a threat to the race itself, or the results, but he had somehow been cast as the villain of the piece, undermining the amateur ideals of the sport, and providing the imperative to exclude him somehow. Hence the refusal to reinstate him, the Lord Mayor's float fiasco, and the endless, microscopic scrutiny at all events, including following cars. It even allegedly extended to tipping off the local constabulary about certain numbers: "Watch them ride; they do this and this; be alert to their law-breaking, and so on."

The North Road win made it clear that Alf had form and strength. He headed for the Perfs Pedal Race, another of his early season leg-testers. Perfs is the historic season opener for most roadmen. It is one of a series of prestigious races, with the Eddie Soens and Severn Bridge road races holding a similar status. Previous winners include Ian Hallam, Sean Yates, Chris Newton and Alex Dowsett. Ian Hallam was looking for a second successive title, but the fearsome track rider, Dave Le Grys, had other ideas. For many, Le Grys is most famous for an appearance on Record Breakers in 1986, riding at 110mph behind a pace car with a fairing. It's terrifying, and to many pre-teen teatime telly watchers in the mid '80s, completely amazing, ensuring instant playground heroic status. He followed this up with a speed record on rollers. It is worth watching just to see what a 232" gear looks like (hint: it involves a chainring the size of a wagon-wheel). Dave was 'quietly confident', whilst Roy Castle looked on in awestruck, benign and confused admiration. The rollers were specially adapted and reinforced.[32] He now runs training camps in Majorca and is a coach and all round good egg. I asked him a question about Alf, and he replied succinctly, "He's my hero. I admired him for three reasons: he was a class tester; he could ride the road and the track as well; and he was a rebel." Le Grys' experience in the 1976 Perfs Pedal Race has a lot to do with it.

"There was a break up the road: Ian Hallam and a couple others had got away; the race was in the balance, if anything it was slipping away. Alf rode up alongside and said, 'Get on my wheel'. It was like being behind a motorbike; he just pulled me across the gap, simple as that. I ended up winning the race in the sprint from Hallam. I was young, just 20 at the time, and forgot to give him any of my winnings. Forty years later I went to the Pedal Club and took the opportunity to stand up and thank Alf – I gave him £15 which was what I received that day. It was an emotional moment."

On 12 June Alf turned up for the '25' championship at Farnham in Surrey, ready to add a sixth cap to his collection. No-one was prepared to bet against him. Eddie Adkins was getting quicker, Mick Ballard was a fine rider, but not a gold prospect, and Roger Queen was also some way adrift. Only Martyn Roach was seen as realistic prospect or outside chance, but after a 3-56 for a hundred miles the week before there were questions over whether he would be sufficiently recovered to mount an effective challenge.

In traditional style, the first rider was off at the inhumanly early time of 6am, but even so a large crowd thronged the start and finish area, with every lay-by filled with men and women armed with stop watches and clipboards, checking the time gaps and craning out into the early summer sun for a glimpse of Alf hurtling past at 30 mph. Many camped overnight to be up and about for the start and a series of overflow car parks were pressed into service to cope with a sea of expectant spectators. It is hard to imagine a similar size of crowd for any event these days, outside of the hill climb. Perhaps something has been lost along the way: personality and difference subsumed beneath technological advancement; human endeavour and frailty negated by wind tunnels; the sight of suffering concealed and the spectacle reduced to a succession of scoring discs slicing or slipping, perhaps, through the air, with each rider hidden beneath a mirrored visor. The narrative and the spectacle have been anaesthetised.

In photos by Phil O' Connor from the Addiscombe TT event on the A2 and Swanscombe Cutting as late as 1982, it is possible to see a sense of equality across the field; disparities in equipment seem minimal. Everyone rides a steel frame made by a South East or London framebuilder: Harry Perry, Chas Roberts, Ken Bird, Holdsworth, Pearson, Geoffrey Butler, Ron Cooper, Roy Thame, Bill Hurlow, Geoff Roberts, Bill Philbrook, Vic Edwards, Witcomb, Condor. The shape and design is the same, only the colours are different.

Exertion is evident through the pained expression on faces. Now we see the management of the external environment and the reduction of the race to qualitative data and numbers, drag and CDA. The two sports are unrecognisable, even as siblings. The cost of amateur competition is enormous. If you want to compete at the sharp end of time trials, it's not enough to be fast, you must match straight line speed with the technological freebies. It's been described as 'free speed', but of course, it is anything but. Every watt increase costs a huge amount of money. Even at inflationary rates, the monetary sums involved are incomparable. Our accessible domestic heroes have been replaced by a professional peloton, a shimmering sight for a few brief seconds, then gone, remaining inaccessible and aloof.

Nowadays, the National '25' is a sparsely attended affair. In 1975, those who loved cycling looked to the pages of *Cycling* to see the exploits of their champions, then ran outside to catch them lined out on an A road near Farnham at 6am in the morning, to mingle, talk and touch them. The weather was murky and still, and the sound of clanking shoe plates and chains whirring carried across on the morning mist to linger with the meandering murmurs of expectation.

> The climax for those starting line worshippers came at seven o' clock, when defending champion Engers' time for waiting was at an end. Before that he had been up and down the main road, circled the immediate starting area, his eyes fixed on some middle-distance target invisible to the onlooker. At one point he crossed Roach, inches away, still warming-up and to start five minutes later. Neither man seemed to see the other, each a prisoner of his own deepening consciousness.[33]

It is a spectacular race report aimed at providing a portrait of the event and the cast list, a narrative of colour, light and texture.

> Then Engers was on the line. The crowd edged closer, somewhere a cine camera whirred. The signal was given and Engers heaved his big gear out into his stride with sudden shouts of 'Come on Alf!' The crowd had at last found its voice for him, as for no other competitor.[34]

Ken Evans captures the status and appeal of Alf in a few short sentences, pinpointing his charisma in words and his endearing role as an iconic and individual folk hero.

The conditions made it hard; like all the nastiest time trials it became a treacly journey through wobbling, viscous molasses. At the ten mile point the damage was done, with Alf half a minute clear of everyone else, including Adkins. He stayed on top of the 118", refusing to change down and churning the huge dinner plate around at a brutal 72rpm. Alf was cheered throughout the ride, and to some consternation again fell victim to following vehicles. A motorbike hovered behind for a few miles, before being moved on by an official, who was of course also following. It had a curious effect on onlookers, and even passing motorists became inhibited by the sight of Alf at full steam, a flash of blue, pedalling at 35mph with the wind.

> I saw him with three miles left to ride, heading a convoy of eight cars preparing to pass yet reluctant to do so, wanting

another close look at this pedalling phenomenon. Clad in Oxford blue, Engers was like a racing eight trailed by powered launches...[35]

The result was a certainty. In true 1970s style, the awards were presented by 'Miss Farnham', in a pair of high-waist corduroy flares and a striped jersey. Alf spoke afterwards to the Comic: "It doesn't get any easier to win, but then the satisfaction is certainly no less than after the first time. Where is the younger challenge though? My closest challenger has been Eddie Adkins, and he's been around a long time. He pushed me hard. I had 'Here comes your nineteenth nervous breakdown' running through my brain. I thought I can't keep winning."

As with previous pre-race nerves, the language is one of mental collapse, the fine line between success and failure and the cost of the level of effort expounded by Alf. Seeking to recast his successes, to cement his reputation, if it needed solidifying, Alf confirmed he would be attempting the BBAR distances of 50 and a 100 miles, along with a 12-hour. The endurance athletes began to shift nervously in their saddles.

Within the month he had served notice of his intent, riding the National '50' Championship in Shropshire. By this point, the Bird bike had changed into a new branded machine. It's barely noticeable amongst the photos, but it crops up here and there: the Intercycle bike. It was an offshoot of the Bird Brothers bike and was finished in the same pale blue as his previous Alec Bird machine.

Alf was involved in the start-up: "This chap, Rob Muir, was interested in cycling, his father was Frank Muir, a cyclist, they had a company called All Type Tools in Woolwich and they made experimental animal cages for the government. Father and son decided that with this factory they were going to go into the cycle business. Frank and Rob used to come into the Bird shop and talked about how they wanted to go into the business, maybe they'd seen a niche and they used Ken and Alec's shop as a launch thing for Intercycle. It was quite messy, but that was how it happened, it was an overlap, the Bird brothers were guiding the project."

"The Bird logo disappeared and they had to think of a new name. Alec said he thought they should come up with the name of a bird. One of the chaps said, 'Susan?' In the end they came up with 'Intercycle' and were hoping to capitalise on the infancy of cycling in America, where there was a bike boom starting. They were exporting frames and they needed a framebuilder. I met them at six o' clock in the morning when they brought this bloke out to an early morning time trial; he was this American representative and they were throwing back gin and tonics, and then being sick in the hedge. They were selling him the idea and he was agreeing to do whatever. They delegated a part of the factory to making these frames.

"At that stage, Ken had the shop and they were both involved with the Muirs using this brand. The bike they came up with I didn't like, so at some stage I had my old Shorter bike with Intercycle transfers on it. I rode an Intercycle, or what looked like an Intercycle, for about a season, certainly no more. Ultimately, the shipments went over, they didn't get the money and the bloke buggered off. Not only that, the frames disappeared as well. That was that. Frank Muir said that the chap involved died in a hotel fire, but apparently he was already dead before the hotel caught fire. That was the story. It got to the beginning of 1978 and I was asking for stuff and it wasn't forthcoming. Two weeks beforehand I'd had a rusty bike, no tyres. The Bird Brothers and the Intercycle thing got very messy so I went back in with Alan Rochford and Alan Shorter. Bill Houghton from the Unity stepped in; he agreed to fund the bike and Alan Rochford built it."

Riding the Intercyle in the '50', Alf was up and ahead by minutes on his nearest challenger, Graham West, and on course for a 1-53 approaching the turn at 40 miles. With a feathering of the brakes and a slight skid the tubular exploded. A spectator, Mick Jeggo, offered a wheel but it wouldn't go in the gap, such were the clearances between seat-tube and tyre, and he gave him the whole bike instead.

Andrew Clarke was marshalling for the Mid-Shropshire Wheelers at the Squirrel Inn final dead turn:

The turn was on a smooth section of road on an open sweeping bend and Alf screamed up, braking late and locking the rear wheel as he slightly overshot the dead turn. Pandemonium broke out. Mick Jeggo tried to change the wheel and Alf eventually rode off on Jeggo's bike. This was about two inches too big for Alf, who was rocking from side to side. Jeggo changed Alf's tub and rode his bike back to the finish with the rest of us. I had a chat with Alf at the finish and he was remarkably philosophical about the puncture. Deep down I guess he blamed himself for maybe not being meticulous in reconnoitring the course beforehand. Anyway he kindly gave this star-struck 17-year-old an autograph and some useful advice on training.

Mick Jeggo's son Nick was also there, an impressionable 14 years old at the time: "We took it in turns to ride Alf's bike back to the finish after fitting a tub. It really felt special, very light and fast for the time, plus it had super light track tubs fitted. It flew! Part of the magic was the fact it was Alf's. Poor Alf had to ride Dad's ancient ex-Falcon team bike.* If he hadn't stood arguing about continuing, he could have still won. He was the only time triallist I really admired and a maverick at odds with the outdated establishment. I think he was a hero to lots of road riders at a time when the sport was quite polarised between 'testers' and road racers."

When I recount this story to Alf, some forty-two years later, he seems flattered and uneasy in equal measure; thrilled that a youngster was so excited to be able to have a go on the best bike in the world, but also uneasy that someone else might have ridden the sacred machine.

Alf had lost time and rhythm, such that Graham West took the title by 30 seconds. Not only that, Alf also missed out on the '25' and '50' double, and knew that it was unlikely he would get another opportunity. It dented his BBAR chances, having missed out on the super-fast Boroughbridge '50' a few weeks earlier.

"The day before the Borough '50' was the Woolwich '25' on the A2. I said to Frank Muir I wanted to do the '50', not the '25'. He said, 'You're going to make me look a bit silly,' so we had to do the '25'. We went to the pub afterwards, and that was that. I said, 'Let's go up to Borough'. But Frank had a report, the weather wasn't good. In any

---

*Mick Jeggo was a highly respected race organiser and friend of cycling, responsible for the long- running Newport Nocturne. He died in 2018, aged 77.

case, they were taking me around everywhere and riding '25's was essential to establishing the Intercycle bike brand. The fastest '25' of the year was always a little square on the front page of *Cycling*. You had to make sure you were the fastest because there was a permanent ad on the front. That was why."

With the BBAR gone, it came down to a single-minded pursuit of the record, with one clear chance in the offing: the A2 course near Swanscombe. It is a fast strip of road with a steady climb up through the Swanscombe Cutting, followed by a very rapid descent. In 1976, it was fair game for a bike race. Nowadays, only those with suicidal tendencies would opt for this stretch of road for a quick blast out and back. It was an evening start, with a sturdy breeze helping the early riders, before easing off by 7pm when Alf lined up for the push, but it was still by no means a float day with the breeze still twitching in the treetops. Mick Ballard was also riding, making the most of a fast evening and aiming for a personal best time at the distance. He went out earlier, but lamented a possible missed opportunity: "I didn't realise how fast it was. I wondered if I had gone hard enough. I had the feeling that I was in for a big hammering." He stopped the clock at 53-40, and immediately got into his car to witness Alf assault the record, eager to see if time trialling history could be made.

Alf knew the road, knew it was fast and knew how to ride it. "I had checked my times previously on that road; the first 5 miles in eight minutes, going through ten miles in 16 minutes or something incredibly fast, because once I got wound up and rolling the gear over I could do it, going really fast for a short period of time, and that road allowed you to do it."

He was also nervous about the wider miasma of suspicion that hung around every event he rode, and opted to be proactive. "At the bottom of the cutting, going up, there was a marshal with binoculars. I asked that person to keep an eye on certain individuals who I knew had perfected a technique of car door handle riding, where they would get onto the car door handle and crouch down and no-one could see them. I caught a very old Ford van just as I was going up and I knew this guy was watching behind because I bloody asked him to watch, and here I was behind this old Ford. So I moved out alongside it and

I went up the Cutting in top gear! The marshal was there watching through binoculars. What could I do, get in behind it? The guy who I'd asked to keep an eye on things was now keeping an eye on me and he ended up putting in a protest."

Alec Bird came along in support. Alf was flying. There is a look and a shape. Ray Pascoe's film 'The King' contains sublime archive footage of Alf at top speed. His body is an oval, knee and thigh in line with forearms, elbows bent. Legs rotate seamlessly, no dead spots, pushing down on the pedals with transcendent efficiency. The upper body moves slightly, shoulders up and down, a nudge, head slightly angled upwards, checking the line of the road, then nodding down, almost imperceptibly, checking the rhythm and cadence, working out the maths. As he powered along the dual carriageway, he was 'on a ride'. The descent of Swanscombe Cutting offered the chance to pick up the pace and grab a handful of seconds as insurance against the drag to the finish. The record was in sight, with a frightening 48-35 pace at the 20 mile mark. Alf had a staggering 90 seconds in hand on the 50 minute barrier, and knew he would hit 55mph on the descent. There was a slight climb to the finish, but it was on. At this point, things became surreal.

"I had an official following me around all the time. If someone got too close to me it'd be toot, toot, toot, toot. I thought, bloody hell, what's all this. He was following me to stop other people following me. You couldn't make it up. I once went to hit him because it was so frustrating and off-putting. The art of time trialling is concentration. It was harassment; I was being harassed on the road."

On this particular day the official was in the lead car with eight following vehicles. Alec Bird was on the hard shoulder, parallel, driving and offering time checks and encouragement.

"I was out in the road. I was bloody terrified, I had 24 spoke wheels on and white strip 2s. We knew there was debris on the inside lane. Originally there was a bloody great door, pieces of wood, rubble, countless other stuff. This builder's open-top lorry had flipped upside down by the petrol pumps at the bottom of Swanscombe Cutting. He had obviously got out of control completely; upside down. And yet nobody else saw it, the debris, the door, the mess. None of the officials. No-one in the eight following cars. I was on 4oz white strip Clement number 2s, ultra light silks with no margin for error, they were my record-ride tyres, on race specials; too bloody right I was in the outside lane. That's what they saw."

Whatever *they* saw, a police car saw the line of eight following cars and Alec Bird on the hard shoulder, shouting encouragement.

"I got to the bottom at 21 miles and they pulled me off the road for 'dangerous riding'. So that was that. It would have been a 48."

I bravely ask him about Alec Bird. It seemed a little incongruous, possibly illegal in motoring terms.

"So how long was Alec Bird on the hard shoulder for?"

"He was on the hard shoulder shouting encouragement and was there the whole of the way down."

"He drove alongside?"

"Yeah. He drove all the way down the cutting. It's a mile long. I got to the bottom and I was pulled off by the police car. Alec had no impact on the race. It was three lanes." Alf is a tiny bit sheepish. I think he is. It's hard to tell because it's not something he does. He confirms my questions.

"It strikes me that Alec Bird driving on the hard shoulder might annoy someone?"

"Well, it was annoying the police car."

Regardless of the legality of Alec Bird shadowing on the hard shoulder – and it doesn't seem to be the best thing to do – the eight following cars elevate the ride into a deranged circus, where Alec Bird's presence off the road is the smallest element of a cavalcade of crazed paranoia and contempt, all unrolling at 30mph on a dual carriageway at 8am. No other rider existed in the same liminal space. The idea of the lone time triallist rolling through in pure solipsism is at odds with Alf's experience every time he took to the road.

The report in the Comic is brief and direct:

"There's no doubt in my mind, this was the night," said a shattered Engers at the finish. Police alleged that he had been riding dangerously on the descent. Organiser Ray Harrad said that there would be an enquiry. "I'm wondering about my cycling career. At 36, what is there left?"

"I was a night baker then. As I went to work that evening, I rang a prominent RTTC official, a friend of mine from the Midlands, and told him what had happened. He said, 'You'll get a two year suspension, down to a year on appeal'."

It was a cruel blow to Alf's hopes and seemed like the culmination of years of challenges, arguments and run-ins with officialdom – many of them petty, but cumulatively enough to destroy the optimism and hopes of even the toughest of competitors.

Alf recounts the charge sheet, 40 years later. "The list goes on. Taking pace. Riding dangerously. Accompanied by a motorbike. Following cars. Wearing a track suit top when cold and not racing. I rode the F1 once. There is a long curve on the F1. One year, somehow they disqualified all the BBAR contestants because they were moving across. One year I got onto this curve, as soon as I did that this police car came up and pushed me off the road. It came to me that the police had special information to keep a look out for number 120. It became a persecution, definitely. At one point I entered a '25' and put my hill climb time on there because it was my last event, but didn't put the point whatever in. I got the entry back with a note: 'Entry returned. Incorrect. Everybody else has taken the trouble to fill it in correctly.' I didn't want to do a hill climb anyway.

"Some of the things were starting to get to me; even riding on the track, if a breakaway gets away it's your duty to chase. On one occasion I was chasing this breakaway, going a lot faster than everybody else, but because I wasn't shoving my shoulders I was pulled out; they said 'You're supposed to take up the chase.' I was flat out! But because I wasn't doing whatever and rolling about with me tongue hanging out I was disqualified. I was in tears. I had had enough of all of them. Whatever I did they were going to find fault. It is intimidating when people are following, and then tell you they are there to help. How are they helping? You tell me. This was absolutely a personal thing. They were telling the police to keep a special watch out for my number. They were absolutely prejudiced; there are no ifs and buts about it. In their head what did they think was going to happen? I even got invited to a club dinner whereupon half the committee threatened to resign. What did they think, that I was a Viking come to rape and pillage? I appeared to be treading on everyone's toes. Am I so different to everyone else?"

The end result of the latest infraction was a two year ban, Alf's third period of time away from the sport he loved: the first time because they wouldn't reinstate him after his 18-month failed stint as an independent; the second time because he was cold and wore a tracksuit top and someone took a photo; and the third time because he was avoiding rubble and a builder's door. It was reduced on appeal to a year, as predicted, as if it was an act of largesse, some sort of bestowing of a favour on the chastened minion by the higher powers. Unsurprisingly, all charges relating to following cars were dropped (they'd be indicting themselves, after all), and the ban reduced to a year based on 'dangerous riding'. Alf gave his views on the hearing in November 1976, as recorded by Ken Evans.

> Engers later said that he had no complaint with the hearing, but charged that he had been 'stitched up'. "Before the original hearing I was told that I would get two years. Before the appeal I was told, from the top, that I would get a year. I race for my own satisfaction, nothing more. If I cheat, then I know I have cheated. On this occasion I know I did not cheat."

I worry about the wording when reading Evans' article. I chew it over. 'On this occasion' – in print it gives the implication that there were other occasions where maybe he'd played a bit fast and loose, over and above any sharp practices which were almost legitimate. I do the only thing I can do and I ask him outright.

"You say I would know if I had cheated. That's about being true to yourself. I get that. Are there any occasions where you did bend or break the rules?"

"Absolutely not. I would know. I did it for myself so I knew I would be cheating myself. I remember once in an open '25' this lorry came by. I accelerated and got on it. As if from above, spokes flew out the rear wheel. But no, never. Not cheating."

"But what about white-lining?"

"Well, I would be erring towards the white line all the time anyway, because that's where the smooth surface is. It wouldn't be in the middle, but it would be out from the kerb. The only cars that built up or came past were because of traffic, for instance the motorbike and side-car. It was a result of the lack of a bypass at Chelmsford on that occasion."

In the immediate aftermath of the hearing he hinted at local prejudice against the Woolwich CC, but also the Barnet. "More than once I got the impression that I was in the wrong club. If they want to, they can get anyone."[36]

Cycling again came out in support of Alf's stance, with a hefty and strident editorial from Ken Evans:

It brings into sharp relief the judiciary problems of the RTTC. Penalties for similar offences vary depending on which DC administrates, and the calibre of the rider involved... In the past we have seen the personal involvement of some DC members result in vicious sentences which have been lightened on appeal. But to lighten them too much would appear disloyal.

Whatever the extent of Engers' guilt or innocence, a sentence of such magnitude should not be the responsibility of local officials whose judgement can often be clouded by personal considerations.

The "Engers affair" has also reflected the jealousy of top riders who, according to any after-race gossiping crowd, stuff themselves full of dope and have a constant stream of following and passing cars whose speed is regulated to induce greater assistance. These top men, so the jealous tales go, are backed not only by men who pay the bills, but who also seek out the right drugs, are highly trained in the surreptitious art of the motor-pace, and who generally connive for their charges to get around the rules of a basically amateur sport. That such talk is rife at and between events reflects badly on time trialling. That such gossip is given voice when a star rider is charged with any offence is equally reprehensible.

Talented riders must be subject to the same regulations as the slowest of long-markers. But similarly, they must be given the same respect. It is time for the RTTC to listen to these whispers, perhaps vicious and unfounded, perhaps based in truth, and take steps to either vindicate star riders or reveal them as cheaters.

It is an unusually forthright statement of the claim and counterclaim swirling around the case. It acknowledges the level of criticism and support for Alf amongst the wider community, but also the wild inconsistencies in RTTC actions. In amongst it is a buried reference to drugs – something that seemed to swirl occasionally around the top competitors, much as it does today. For instance, hearsay emerged in 1968, gossip and innuendo surrounding the '25' Championship near Manchester won by Ray Ward with Mummery and Engers tied for second. In a later interview Alan Gayfer addressed the question directly with Alf, who responded in kind. "I don't think there are many men in time trialling who would stoop to taking dope. How much does a good dope test cost anyway? I would welcome a dope test after the championship."[37]

I raise the issues with Alf regarding the whispers. "Allegedly somebody found a hypodermic around, which could have been anything," he said. "Even now there are whispers when someone comes up without any other superb rides and then does a superb ride, and there were riders who that happened to. There was a lot of innuendo about drugs, a lot around me as well. Maybe it's par for the course. When I came back, they were all taking this tonic called Metatone.* Everybody was taking it at the time. I took it. It was horrible; it was so horrible I thought it must be doing good. Apparently it had point whatever of strychnine in it."

Cycling's editorial also hints at personal grudges, the desire for one district to enact a process and persecute a rider. Evans addresses the gossip, the sour grapes that accompany victory, and especially repeated victory, but urges the RTTC to take some sort of definitive action. It is a world of parochialism and petty persecutions, of conflict between personality, charisma, success and authority. It is a reflection of everything that we love to hate about cycling, and as an editorial would be applicable to almost any story of success in cycling before or after, whether it's Choppy Warburton, Tom Simpson or Bradley

---

* An over-the-counter tonic, still widely available, still disgusting.

126

Wiggins. Skulduggery, injustice and hyperbole transcend time, we just don't realise when we're immersed in our silent emasculation of the latest sporting demi-god. From our armchairs we stick the knife in. We then wait for rehabilitation and our chance to confirm speciously that we loved them all along.

For Alf, there was a very human cost. He was 36 years old and faced with another period of inactivity. Not only was he fighting a battle against time, the unceasing search for seconds and pace, but also the nagging anxiety that he was getting older and it was only going to get more difficult. He was crushed by the ruling, the process, and the outcome, regardless of the reduction to a year. He wanted to 'abdicate' the '25' title he had won in June, seeing it as one and the same.

"I rode exactly the same way and if they can disqualify me on one occasion they should have done so on the other. As far as I'm concerned, Eddie Adkins is the champion." The bit that really stuck in the craw was the one item left on the charge sheet: 'taking pace from a motor vehicle' on the descent of the Swanscombe Cutting; "That's the one place you wouldn't need pace! I was passing the traffic down there!"

The ever empathetic Ted Kings expressed his reservations when Alf announced both his 'abdication' and that he would not be attending the end of season bean-feast, also known as the 'Champions' Dinner'. "I hope he does come to the national dinner, if only for the sake of his team mates and the 800 or so others who will be there."

His reaction at the time was simple: "I shall be writing to decline all my dinner invitations. I don't want to hear the word 'bike' for another 200 years."

He went fishing.

Lesson ƐI

The better rides are easier

Being used to enforced absences doesn't make them any easier, especially when it involves both authority and the fickle and grasping fingers of time in a wide-ranging conspiracy, seemingly designed to take away the one goal Alf had left to achieve. Throughout 1977 the glowering spectre of Alf lurked on the sidelines, a malevolent and maligned presence. His record of victories remained a benchmark out of reach by the chasing pack, and his record set in 1969 seemed no closer to being overturned by any of the new breed of fast young gunslingers. Nevertheless, his absence from the Championship meant a new champion, and for many, Eddie Adkins was the president-elect. Derek Cottington had never recaptured his initial burst of form, the proverbial candle burning twice as brightly, and Roger Queen was there to provide the test.

Adkins was (and still is) a favourite of many. Unmistakeably one of the good guys, riding for VC Slough, he was quiet and reserved, the typical silent assassin in many ways. His teammate Roger Queen was optimistic that under the auspices of the silver jubilee it might be his turn. Phil Griffiths was the outsider, a teammate of Joe Waugh at GS Strada Lutz and every inch the international roadman, with a yellow jersey in the Peace Race in 1973, silver in the '74 Commonwealth Games road race, he won prolifically at the highest level, including the 1976 Olympics. Furthermore, he had form, having won the BBAR for the previous two years. Many thought he was more than an outside bet for the title.

All the while, Engers lurked silently, watching and absorbing the details, offering advice to those who asked, watching some more, commenting on Griffiths' equipment choices. "I had chosen white-strip silk tubulars, so light even Alf hadn't seen them before. Then he told me that they had to be fitted in a certain way, and in any case they were risky. So instead of riding 24s and white strips, I ended up on training wheels with 36 spokes." Alf's word seemed law.

It was another scenic stretch of concrete between Newark and Grantham. Competitors were greeted by a malicious, swirling wind, slicing across the course and giving no help, except in the last few miles. Huge chainrings on the way out led to even lower cadences, sub 20mph at 70rpm, until finally, at around 18 miles, the direction shifted and all 57 teeth could be bared in anger. It crushed the lighter riders, who were buffeted and assaulted by the wind, whilst the bigger beasts laboured heavily but held their course, like lumbering oil tankers rumbling up to speed.

Adkins' position was perfect, his hair neatly parted by the force of the wind, hands on the low brake levers, saddle high, long legs stretched out and pedalling in eerily perfect circles. Griffiths had ridden hard into the wind, hitting the first ten miles in 22-29, with Roger Queen just ahead in 22-22. Adkins was half a minute back, with time checks coming thick and fast from supporters on the road. The promoting club had laid miles and miles of telephone cable to ensure accurate and fast reporting of the times to the HQ. It was quite an effort. At the turn the big gears took over. Adkins spun the plate with ferocity and began an inexorable march towards the title, stealing seconds with each turn of the pedals. Griffiths was unable to cope with the specialists, losing 20 seconds to Queen and nearly a minute to Adkins in the last 5 miles alone. The after-effects of a heavy cold and a job lot of penicillin ("I took all my doctor had") didn't help. In the end it was as predicted, but the margin was tight: Adkins first in 56-00, an indication of the slowness of the day, with Roger Queen a meagre 3 seconds back, then Griffiths at 56-42. Compensation for Griffiths came in the form of a third BBAR title by the end of the year. For Adkins, Alf or no Alf, he had a shiny cap and his name in the book, and knew it was going to be a lot harder next year.

Having decided to return in 1978, there were two priorities for Alf: as well as doing more speed work and less volume, he needed a new bike. Alf was becoming obsessed with smoothing out the airflow in order to enable the bike to slip through the air. During his year out something he had seen in the late 1950s resurfaced from the depths of his memory. He recalled seeing an experimental machine put through its paces at Herne Hill.

"It was called the Sputnik after the first satellite in space. It was an ordinary bike encased in a cigar tube. That bike, with an average rider, beat the England pursuit team on a 4000 metre pursuit. One of them was Tommy Simpson. It was obvious then, in the 1950s, that it was the way forward, but no-one could afford wind tunnels so things stayed the same and people forgot about it. When I read about it recently, they were saying fibreglass, but I remember it as alloy. It looked like a bubble car."

He knew then, but somehow the knowledge or the connection lay dormant, an ember glowing in the recesses of the mind and an idea ahead of its time. The demise of Intercycle and the Bird brothers meant a frame needed building, a post-drillium speed machine. Assistance was provided by Alan Rochford and Alan Shorter. Initially, he went to see Ron Cooper, one of the best London framebuilders who had served his apprenticeship with A.S. Gillott in 1947. He set up on his own in 1967 in Honor Oak Park, building by hand without a frame jig. He had learnt from H.E Green and Jim Collier, master builders from the pre-war era, and certainly knew how to race, having ridden the Tour of Britain in 1952. Despite Cooper's pedigree, Alf found it difficult to get him to understand exactly what he wanted. "They just couldn't seem to get their head around building a track bike for the road. I went to see Ron Cooper. I didn't tell him who I was, but he knew bloody well who I was. I said, 'Ron I want a six day bike to ride on the road. Everything really really close'.* He said, 'Come back in two weeks and I'll show you what I have done.' I turned up and he showed us what he had made, and said, 'I don't want anyone else's name going on it because I spent a lot of time on it.' Essentially, it was a Belgian road bike and not a track bike for the road. I didn't want a Belgian road bike. I said to Ron, 'Er... I'll come back to you on it.' At that point we realised Barry Chick (working in the Shorter shop, and a member of the Barnet) could probably build what I wanted, because it wasn't something particularly special, just an out-and-out track bike. Barry did it as I wanted it. Ron didn't do it. I guess with his experience

---

* 6-Day Track bikes were very tight, with 'fag-paper' clearances between wheel and fork crown/seat-tube. Hetchins produced one with a fluted seat-tube to bring the wheel in.

130

he probably thought, 'You don't want this; I'm going to build you the frame that you want even though you think you don't want it. He can't want that, he'll never turn it, he'll get toe overlap'."

"The first of the machines made by Barry was tight. I mean, it was so tight, practically inventing Rizla paper clearance. We were starting to think about the frame design and shape, and less about the holes. Barry made the bike, Old Al put it together. They were nothing like the Bird brothers, put it that way. They used to have these cups in the bottom brackets that were always coming loose. Old Al had a way to cure that. He'd turn the bike upside down and wallop it with a sledgehammer. The bloody thing splayed right out. It certainly stopped it coming out."

The components were adapted, milled and polished by Alan Lear, then a Lampard RC clubman and engineer. Barry Chick opted for Columbus *Pista Leggera* tubing, the preferred steel for pursuit frames or hour records, and went for a Super Vitus rounded fork blade – the type seen on sprinter's machines – on account of reduced air flow. The fork crown was milled back and reduced, again with air flow in mind. The cabling was hidden and ran underneath the frame, with a single boss for the downtube lever. The lever in turn was buffed to within an inch of its life, a Campagnolo shifter married to a Sachs-Huret Jubilee rear derailleur. Alan Lear had rounded every edge and trimmed the derailleur, giving it a pure and organic form. Even the chainring was 'thinned' with the rear supports removed and every angle or bump reduced to nothing. Super Record pedals were brutally de-quilled and toe straps cut to measure. After previous issues with drilled seatposts, the Laprade post was reamed out and tentatively tightened to avoid collapse. "If you looked at the bike it was bog standard, but everything on it was adapted. The seatpost slipped down because it was hollow, the handlebars moved, you were only ever a couple of pedal strokes from it falling apart."

The bars were utterly denuded; they were a classic Cinelli Stem and 64 combination which had been welded together to avoid using a stem bolt. It's the purest incarnation of marginal gains; anything that could go, could be replaced, or could be altered was attacked with the workshop tools. The most eye-catching element were the brakes. They went for a set of Weinmann 605 because the right hand pull meant the front could be placed carefully between the fork crown and downtube. A pair of polished, shiny, stripped and milled levers were placed behind the tops, like reverse suicide levers, facing backwards. They were invisible from the front. Even the journalist at the Comic was a bit freaked out by this: "We have some reservations about the extra time needed to reach for the levers, but the brakes do work normally – and can even respond to pressure from the forearms at times."[38] The idea of hurtling down a slope at 55mph and then using forearms to feather the brakes ahead of a roundabout turn is at best brave, at worst suicidal.

The rims were Arc-En-Ciel 24 spoke. It's worth mentioning that these are absurdly light. I used a pair on the Rake in the National Hill Climb in 2012. That's how light they are, even now. Hubs were made by Omas and spindles were titanium. It is a frightening manifest of high-end late 70's bike smut. It was built for one thing and one thing only: straight-line speed. It couldn't be ridden on technical courses or grippy road surfaces. With a wheelbase of 36 inches every striation on the surface of every grain of gravel was transmitted up through the forks. Turning was a challenge, with significant toe overlap always a risk. It was a bike for sitting down. No standing efforts of any length were permitted; the potential for the house of cards to collapse was ever-present.

Unsurprisingly, the bike turned heads whenever it made an appearance. But it came with a stern and portentous note of warning: 'Lightening standard components is a skilled task and should only be carried out by a qualified person. Even then there could be breakages because some of the components may be already built to the limit of lightness. This particular rider pedals smoothly, for instance, and a different type of rider, more jerky perhaps, could end up breaking something.'[39]

Within a month the RTTC had acted to outlaw the positioning of the brake levers; they had to go back onto the widest point of the bars. But apart from that, it was the same bike. He would ride the Mk 2 Speed Machine at the '25' Championship in June and mapped out the rest of the season, confident he had the bike to match his ambitions.

Ahead of the new season, Alf kept his counsel, replying in enigmatic epithets to questions from the press in early January 1978; "I shall ride the odd event. After a year off, strange things can happen. You can say, 'I'm over the top. It's a trip down memory lane.' I've not too much ambition."

With five months to go before the '25' Championship, he was steadily building up form, with an entry in for the Perfs Road Race. Glenn Longland got away to win by over two minutes with Dave Le Grys, John Herety and Alf the next three riders. Things were looking up, and people were getting agitated. He had a good run in the lead up to the Championship on 10 June. With Roger Queen, Martin Pyne and Eddie Adkins lined up, it promised at least to ask the question as to who was the fastest, if not confirm the answer. After a year out, and having just turned 38, the questions over Alf's longevity swirled around. King of the unusual simile, Dennis Donovan, did the honours for *Cycling*:

> Engers circled the road a few times, staring ahead intently as the crowd looked at him and the famous 'speed machine'. Someone told this reporter that he had written a lot of 'rubbish' in his preview. Engers took almost a run at the start, stopping just enough for the last ten seconds to be intoned by timekeeper Frank Minto, then melted into the distance like the last ice cream on earth.

Alf blasted out of the blocks, stealing 11 seconds by halfway. From thereon in, things went adrift. Adkins rode another perfectly paced 25, whilst Alf faded, finishing 16 seconds down in fourth place. Mick Bradshaw managed third with Martin Pyne in second. Catching up with Mick, 40 years later, he recalled the event in technicolour. "He was such a presence at the race and it lifted everybody's game when you saw his name on the start sheet. The '78 champs was one of the closest finishes ever. Thinking back I had to laugh 'cos every mile or so down the course there was a cockney type voice shouting at me, 'Yer down on Engers.' It just made me go faster; nothing to do with Alf, just over-eager supporters. At the end I was stood on a beer crate next to Eddie and Martin for the photos."

It was far from a fairytale return, but the tightness of the title race suggested all was not lost. The headwind had dented the aspirations of many, with Roger Queen taking a royal battering. Alf was sanguine about the result, even quite pleased with his ride. "In the '25' Championship I'd gone too fast, too soon, mainly because I thought, 'this bloody Eddie, let's make some time up on him.' That's what I was trying to do. It didn't work. I couldn't have beaten Eddie Adkins in the Championship. I wasn't on form. It was a hot day and I remember asking for a drink, which I never would have done on a short distance time trial."

Adkins had confirmed his status as the fastest 25-miler and had done something very few riders had done before – beaten Alf Engers in a big event. It was an achievement which garnered respect. Even so, the margins were slim, 16 seconds is a clear win, but not definitive, and Alf headed away with one thought in mind – closing out the season with the relentless pursuit of the record, the final feather in his cap. He got his head down, rode and raced, and fixated on the warmth of August and the season-ending fast events.

Come 5 August, 1978, and the summer sun had settled on the tarmac. Long, balmy summer days and high air pressure tempted the testers; the high point every season for records, where the weather and form can occasionally combine to create glorious float days. Eddie Adkins, Alf Engers, Mick Ballard, Roger Queen, Glenn Longland, Granny West and Mike Burrow all headed out to the E72 in search of fast times and glory. It was the fastest field assembled since the national and a straight-out slugfest beckoned, attracting big crowds, eager to see something special, and baying for a competition record. It was now or never for Alf.

"I had done a night shift and there was some time in between because I'd finished work at around 3am. I'd rushed through to finish early, even though Friday night is the busiest for a baker. I ate a tin of rice and a couple of cheese rolls, washed down with some black coffee, then I set off. I would do that now if I was racing.

"I drove out there with Judith, eating some mint cake on the way. We had been together for less than a year. We had met in a wine bar in Highgate in 1977. Judith already had a feel for what was going on with people. At one point, for example, Doug Brunwin said that she was a following car. She had driven down the road to give me a time on the way back, so she was therefore a following car. There was always this sense of sour grapes, of being in the wrong club, getting on the wrong side of the North London Mafia. Doug Brunwin and the Brentwood CC held an annual event which was seen as the blue riband event at the end of every year, really fast and really prestigious. That's where Dave Dungworth got the competition record and they stoked that reputation. However, I didn't like the Southend road anymore. I said to the press, 'Nobody rides that event anymore, if you want to do a fast time, that isn't a fast event.' That year entries were down for Doug Brunwin. They weren't happy about it."

Adkins was in-form and the two heavyweights were separated by ten minutes on the card, with Adkins off first, and Alf as scratch. The initial plan was for an evening event, but London East had concerns about the amount of cars on the road, so requested an early start instead. Inevitably, "all hell was let loose in the morning; you should have seen the traffic," according to Bill Houghton, the Unity CC sponsor. Records began to fall almost immediately: Dave Worsfield rode his tricycle round in 57-38, a Ben-Huresque 26mph ride. The junior record was next to be rearranged by Tim Stevens, a beanpole of a South Londoner, who went round in 53-18. The juvenile record also fell, along with the team record. It left only the battle for individual honours.

"At the HQ I heard that three women had beaten the hour. I'd warmed up and was ready. I looked for signs that would indicate super form, but there were none. Instead, I had an incredible and inexplicable feeling of well-being. All that I could do had been done. I taped over the lace eyelets on my shoes as the final touch, and was ready.

"At the start you only had to go a few hundred yards out and over this flyover and back. At that point I could hear the grit on the tyres. I was riding small-flange 24s with a 13-14-15 block and a 57 ring on the front. I felt I would be able to ride the 13 up the hills. Alan Rochford took the 12 off, which in retrospect I could have probably turned over. This was before the Chelmsford bypass was built, so you had these big queues of traffic stood still going through Chelmsford like a road block, so they then began coming in droves: a big load of traffic, then nothing at all; then the same thing again. That was the case on this particular day when I got out onto the carriageway. It was one of those times."

Alf sighs, audibly, I hear it in the room and I hear it again listening back to the recording. A pause, an intake of breath, a formless noise that speaks of a moment of reflection, an emotion rising to the surface, like a sullen carp emerging from the depths of the murky lake of memory, from inchoate form to shape and substance, before gulping air and sinking noiselessly back down into the abyss of time. An impossible moment to transcribe, where somehow silence and then sound is freighted with much more meaning than the words that follow.

"I could feel that I was going to be as good as I could be. I knew it on this occasion. When I got pulled off the road at Swanscombe I had it. It happened on the A2 on two occasions, the first time I punctured, the second time the police stopped it. If you can describe it, you are out of your body, somehow or other, and there is a fluid, effortless grace. For the most part, the better rides are easier; it's the slower rides where you have really got to slog. When it's there, you just fly.

"It had been raining, there was a light wind. There has to be a wind drift of some description. I've long thought that because of the proximity of the E courses to the sea that the sea has a bearing on it, on the wind, the atmosphere, and the amount of oxygen in the air. I've also been of the opinion that your body is on a four week cycle, very good, not so good, down and then back up again. It seemed very fast, even going into the wind. Then it started to rain quite hard, which would allay the wind, so it made sense to get to the turn as quickly as possible.

"In my mind's eye I felt perfectly relaxed and yet at the same time, aware of absolutely everything. I was controlling myself from within, as if I was the driver of an alien force, deciding if and when more power should be turned on, perfectly relaxed, yet at the same time aware of everything.

"That is it. Where we go from there I don't know."

Adkins reached the 'long' turn in 26-08, leaving 9 miles left to ride. It was record pace, and well beyond 30mph average. Adkins was on fire. He knew it and the spectators knew it. The crowd waited for Alf's time to come in. He was four miles back down the road. Time checks from the turn clocked Alf at a scarcely believable 25-05, averaging 35mph with the breeze, and reaching 40mph at times on the way out, turning over a top gear of 118". The wind eased a little and the rain stopped at the turn.

"I overtook a couple of vehicles, and could see a solid block of traffic. Behind it was the same. Descending the turn, I engaged the 13 and stayed on it for the rest of the ride. During the descent I thought what might happen if I burst a tyre, then decided it wasn't worth worrying about because I would be a dead man ten times over.

"I was overtaking solid lines of holiday traffic, and as the road flattened they started to catch up, but up ahead was another solid block of cars across both lanes. It was in and around the finish area, where we rode through before the last turn. There was a grassy bank where they were all standing and looking at the finish seeing the riders coming by. I could see the crowd and hear them as I crossed the line. As I was riding I looked ahead and I could see that I was catching all this traffic up, there was a motorbike and sidecar out in the lane and I was coming up on them. And I knew they were all on this bank and I could hear them. I was on the outside of this traffic, and I just thought, 'Look at that! What am I going to do? Get in behind it?' The dilemma was whether to stay where I was, and risk breaking regulation 48, or to get off the road.

"In that moment I knew that there could be a problem, but I couldn't do anything about it. I'd gone as hard as I could possibly go, and I'd gone too fast too soon and I was really struggling to get back. I was acutely aware that people were just watching to say 'Well...' A handful of spectators put their own slant on the race, which had a devastating effect later on.

"At the top of the course, for the last turn, Bill Houghton gave me a time check, I was up 1-30 on Adkins. The wind hadn't completely dropped, but it was possible to cut through it, a thin air day. On reflection, on the previous occasions I have broken the record, the same type of conditions prevailed; always dull and stormy, plenty of oxygen in the air. Heavy traffic alone is not enough. At six miles out it was ideal, but there was a drag and I knew I had to hold on in the 13."

Adkins crossed the line in 50-50, breaking Alf's nine year old competition record. He had blitzed the course and the existing mark. The record was finally his. All he had to do was wait and see if Alf could beat it. The crowd knew the record had fallen, and knew they had only nine minutes to wait to see if things changed further. A subdued tension hung in the air. Necks craned, each one keen to be the first to get a glimpse of Alf, to confirm the sighting and send the murmuration outwards, down the line in fluttering oscillations of excitement. They looked down and along the greying concrete waiting to see a form and shape emerge from the pulsing patterns of heat and light dancing over each car.

"People were saying 'It's on!' 'What's on?' Jack Lacey had a sign up saying the same. I mean, Eddie said the same thing about his race. All I was thinking then was that I wasn't going to get back. Right at the end of the race I got out of the saddle and I knew that was wrong, because the bike would drop to pieces, and it pretty much did. The back wheel went out of true and I had to sit down quick. If I'd have kept on, it would have disintegrated.

"I went up over the last rise with just the slip road to go. The marshals at the top were going mad, waving their arms. I got a shout of '48 minutes' from Mike Gambling, and in the distance I could see the finish. Everything went blank. The crowd were cheering and clapping, people were running. I retched and threw up, but there was nothing to throw up. The only time I get something like that is when I'm around 51 minutes. So I hoped I'd done well enough. I didn't know, you can't know, I mean. Alan ran up to me and kissed me, and said, 'You've done it, a forty-nine'.

"It was over. Ten years of trying, the disappointments, the bad luck, were over. I looked at the sky, expecting to hear a heavenly chorus. Instead, somewhere, a dog barked. I wasn't actually living with me wife then, I went home to the first wife. I picked up me fishing rods. I told her, 'I've done a 49.' She said straightaway, 'They'll find something wrong with it.' And she was right.

"I went to see me mother and then I went fishing."

It was a 49, but it was much more than that. To be precise, it was 49-24, an incomprehensible time. It was a massive margin, eclipsing Eddie Adkins' ride by nearly 90 seconds. It was the culmination of years of effort and an unrelenting battle with authority. It was an end to everything – all the questions, the desire for success and for recognition, the fanaticism, the lot. But, as predicted, within minutes of the mark being set it was being challenged. Yet again, the miasma of suspicion emanated from the London East District officials, a toxic cloud of intent rumbling into a thunderstorm of anger and bitterness.

"I knew it was a fast day, so I rode guardedly, making sure, as I thought, that no-one could challenge my claim to the record. I even came away from the event thinking that everything was ok, and that I'd done the fastest ride of my life. It wasn't until the next day when Mr Brunwin was rounding people up, waking them from their beds, to say the record didn't stand."

A familiar name led the inquisition. Doug Brunwin gave his view in the Comic:

> I was not at the event on Saturday. On Sunday, at the Southend '50', I was inundated with queries on what I was going to do about Engers' riding the day before. Several said he was riding in the centre of the road and the traffic was building up behind him. Though no complaints were made on the spot, two written complaints from District Council members were forwarded on to me and the number of verbal complaints was quite substantial.
>
> The complaints will have to be dealt with by the promoting club – and Engers is a member of that club – or an enquiry can be held. It's difficult to prove cases like this, but he has been suspended before for this type of riding and I've been told there was a two and quarter mile queue of traffic at one time behind him. It would seem terrible if we approved a competition record under these circumstances.

It is evident from the comments that Brunwin's stance was to assume guilt, prior to any enquiry or report, and to imply strongly that the record should not be ratified. The prehistoric wheels of RTTC justice began turning in addled circles, and the record went unratified. The promoting club, Unity Hireconomy, held an enquiry. Promoter Barry Freeman referred to a lack of any reports from observers posted on the course, and he requested sight of the written complaints that Brunwin had spoken of. They decided there was no case to answer. Brunwin's use of emotive language and citing of 'previous' seemed designed to ensure one outcome.

For Alf, it was simple: nothing had changed. He knew what had happened in and amongst the heavy holiday traffic. "I was keeping to the side as much as possible; going down Hatfield Peverel hill I overtook some cars which were going slower than I was. Then when I started going up the other side, they started overtaking me again. There's nothing you can do about a situation like that. If I'd stayed behind them then I might have been accused of taking pace. It's like being in a condemned cell. I don't think I did anything wrong, but talk of a two and a half mile tailback is ridiculous. At no time did I cross the white line, and in any case, there were police all over the place. I feel sure they would have stopped me if I had."

There followed a six-month wait while the saga played out.

"I thought, 'I'm not going to ride anymore; enough is enough, and I've had a lifetime of tussling with these people.' I was riding for myself, for my own satisfaction, so if I'd have paced I'd have known. There was nothing wrong."

Having heard the outcome of the enquiry, Brunwin and London East were clearly unhappy, and thus decided to hold their own enquiry. In response to this unusual step, the national body stepped in (Rule 45(c)) to take control of proceedings at the request of Unity CC, and 'in the interest of the sport'. Dudley Roberts, Chair of the RTTC nationally, took charge: Engers and his solicitor sat on one side, with Brunwin and Bill Thorncroft from London East on the other. Roberts listened to the submissions and called the witnesses, before dismissing all charges. This second enquiry confirmed Alf's fourth competition record, with the first being in 1959, a slightly demented 19 years prior. Ken Evans in *Cycling* came down resolutely in favour of the ruling: "We applaud the initiative of the RTTC... Such is the strength of feeling against the officials of London East (and indeed South East) where Engers has been in trouble before... a bold step by the RTTC."[40] Evans followed it up with a neat summary of Alf's struggles: "He was the target of small minds; a martyr to his own charisma."

At the end of the season Alf headed to the Champions' Dinner to receive the special gold medal from the RTTC for the first 30mph ride. Mick Bradshaw had made the trek down from the North East to collect his bronze medal from the '25' Championship: "All these old blokes turned up on bikes, disappeared into the toilets then came out with tuxes on. They were mumbling that Alf shouldn't be receiving a medal, how it wasn't a proper ride, blah blah blah. I'd won three medals that year, so I got well blasted. I was already a little bit pissed by then and politely told them to go forth and multiply in the Geordie vernacular. I'm sure I got invited to a party at Alf's later, but was so pissed I got lost. The bright lights and big city and a northern country boy were a bad mix."

As for Alf, in 2018?

"As far as I know London East still don't recognise the record."

Lesson 14

What else can you do, but go fishing?

All of the singular determination and fanaticism involved in the ceaseless desire to ride faster and defeat time evaporated at the second the clock stopped. All talk of rivals, controversy, of change and slowing down, ended. Ambivalence was suddenly limited to the historical record; Alf had achieved what he set out to do, something no-one else could do ever again.

"It was done. I didn't want to ride anymore: there was nothing left to do. There is this strange anticlimax where it doesn't feel like you thought it should. It's like wanting to shag Mick Jagger. Eventually you shag Mick Jagger but then you complain that it's not like Mick Jagger. The four-minute mile was my analogy; in my head, that was the way I saw it, that and the four-hour hundred. Roger Bannister and Ray Booty can only ever be the first people to do it. It was a record I wanted; I wanted to be the only person ever to have done it. I had a vague sense of anticlimax which I wrote about at the time: the absence of the heavenly chorus, instead, a dog barking. It was a hazy day. What else can you do but go fishing?"

Alf withdrew his entries and all but ceased riding. The record was finally "where other blokes couldn't get it"; a statement cruelly enforced by the sudden and total eclipse of Adkins' new competition record. On the best day, with the best form, riding to the conditions, within the letter of the law, Alf had conclusively proved that no-one was remotely anywhere near. In fact, they were, at the very least, 1,408 yards further back down the road. That was in the case of Eddie Adkins, the second fastest man in history; everyone else was a lot further back still.

He didn't hang up his shoe plates entirely; he made periodic appearances at events, including the National, on a couple of occasions. In 1982 he managed a shortish 52 minute '25'. It's tempting to wonder why he emerged to have another go. In short, he felt like he had the legs, commenting at the time, "The riders at the top are not as good as they should be. I'm glad to see Dave Lloyd back and it's a step in the right direction. I'm pleased that he won and not one of the current cowboys. It's not a wholehearted thing as far as I'm concerned. I can't do the training."

He disappeared again for a few years, before emerging out of the gloaming to ride the National again in 1985 having been tempted out of retirement by Phil Griffiths, who had invited him to join the GS Strada because he admired his unreconstructed charisma and style. "Alf wore a fur coat, way before rock stars, right down to the ground, sitting in the back of a big Jag with an earring, came out with a bike like a guided missile."[41] Even at the Leicester track some years before, Griffiths had greeted Alf with the words; "the man who put the P in poser." He finished outside the top 20 whilst Darryl Webster took his second title. The shift to aero had gathered pace, with 24" wheels on the front and upturned cowhorns adorning most of the race weaponry. By then Alf was 45 and not clinging on to be an all-conquering supervet like Woodburn or Adkins. He was done with it.

Adkins and Queen also rode, as did his old sparring partner Martin Pyne, and John Woodburn finished in 14th. By the mid 1980s the profile of the sport seemed to be shifting: veterans were holding on for longer, achieving more, the average age of competitor was increasing. Webster seemed to be a new variant on a theme, with *Cycling* labelling him as a 'firebrand'. He was, and still is, admired by Alf, then as a young uncompromising rider, streets ahead of the competition, entirely uninhibited and willing to speak his mind, now as an outsider, someone who fought the same fight and empathises with the struggle. Like Alf, he seemed to do things on his own; he was a solipsistic character who didn't need the approbation or acceptance of others; he rode for himself, with a certain strength of character and self-belief that he could do better than everyone else. Webster is open and generous in his assessment of Alf:

"My earliest memory of him was at the Rainbow Rooms in London for the RTTC dinner. He was there to collect his medal for the first sub 50 min '25'. I was there as GHS* winner in 1978. He had some

---

* National Schools 10-Mile Championship, named after George Herbert Stancer.

kind of Robin Hood green, flared jumpsuit on. There must be a picture somewhere of him from that night.

"Before the 1985 Champs I stayed at Alf's house. Harry Whinlow (a former Bradgate RC clubmate who used to come to the championships with me to prepare my race bike while I warmed up on my road bike) also stayed over, and it was a real highlight for him because Alf was his hero. To enjoy his hospitality and meet him in that type of situation was a great moment for him. We all laughed a lot that night. Alf disappeared very quickly after his ride the next day. He was off to try and catch a mythical carp somewhere nearby.

"He's far more of a hippy than most grasp and definitely the first rock star of time trialling. He was ahead of his time regarding intensity over duration. The only other rider of the era to get this right was probably Ian Hallam. I think but for his knee cap problem he might have gone down the route of road racing a lot more, and been quite a formidable roadman. That said, he might well have struggled with the attitude of many roadmen towards testers. They are a sarcastic bunch to say the least.

"He is something of a kindred spirit. We're both anti-establishment, cynical of government and to some degree we are loners. I think Alf's perhaps more introverted, despite the extrovert image. I doubt he'd admit it but I'm sure he cultivated the image to some degree and revelled in his notoriety."

I find myself wondering if Webster also revels in the notoriety; it's back to the same idea expressed in the prologue of this book. After a while, being true to yourself becomes a badge of honour of sorts. Life is built on compromises, both appropriate, and sometimes less so, but nearly always born of necessity. Without compromise things are immeasurably more difficult, but also more simple.

Without the endless pressure and internecine squabbles, Alf was able to take time out. He went fishing, and then he began thinking about the new and slightly crazy world of triathlon. It represented a break from the past, with the tantalising prospect of a blank canvas."I liked the idea of this new sport with these new people coming in. The hierarchy and whatever else I was enduring did not exist in triathlon as such. There were rules, but it was a lot of people coming from different backgrounds; their preparation was different from what the cyclists were doing. They were doing things like the Lydiard style, intervals, a pyramid*, and there weren't all these bloody officials waiting to tell you that you hadn't done this and you hadn't done that, and for the first time I didn't have to win.

"I was competing all over the place. Imagine somewhere in Yorkshire; getting in a river at eight in the morning and swimming down river, or at the docks with 600 others. A lot of them were open water. I was Vets champion but you were never ever going to beat the swimmers because they were good at everything, whereas cyclists can only ride bikes. I coached the Olympic swim captain to ride and he'd coach me with swimming, but I can't point me toes because I always held my foot in position, as a result your hamstrings are shortened. The only way to do it was to stand on a wobble board. I had a bit of that but I thought, 'Hang on a minute, you're 40-odd and going to do something silly.'

"When I was a triathlete, we got an invitation to take part in an ad for Midlands Electricity Board. There were two actors on a tandem, and a whole heap of cyclists chasing them. The pack was made up of Tour of Britain riders, professionals, with amateur triathletes making up the numbers. It got very messy. The triathletes were crashing into the Tour of Britain riders, the actors on the tandem fell off; it was chaos. Thursday we did the next shoot; we got togged up, grey suits, bowler hats. A group of kids saw us and said, 'What a bunch of wankers.' That was that, really."

And still his 1978 record stood. Riders came and went, and none came remotely near it. Ten years later, in 1988, Alf had another go at the National on the back of his triathlon form. He looked incredible, like some sort of prototype Cippolini by way of Barnet. He had ridden for North London CC, a club which seems to have disappeared almost as quickly as it arrived, and then joined the Total Fitness Triathlon team. Always one for the understated entrance, Alf turned up wearing a full-body, purple and blue hooped skinsuit. The helmet was an early Assos aero lid with a science-fiction visor. It was nicknamed 'the fairy suit' and it made for quite a spectacle.

---

* Arthur Lydiard pioneered training in phases and peaking for specific races.

That was as good as the race got. He went off course at the far turn: "I was expecting people to point and they didn't. Maybe subconsciously I didn't want to do it. I had it half in the back of my mind, and I rode another one up here and the same thing: I saw someone coming back down towards me. And I thought, 'I don't want to do this'. I remember the last race I did. It was bloody snowing, April 1989 and I rode through the start line and someone told me I'd be reported to London East because I'd done this, or that. I undid the toe-straps and went home."

It wasn't until 1990 that international roadman Pete Longbottom finally beat the mark by a meagre 11 seconds, with a smattering of new aerodynamic weapons, including a disc wheel. By the following year, with the ratification of tri-bars, the sport changed forever. Chris Boardman became the first to break 48 minutes in 1992 using a Mavic disc, front tri-spoke and aero-bars. It was the same year he won the Olympic Pursuit on a Lotus. A brief glance at photos from the era show the extent of the positional changes and appliance of technology. Alf is not dismissive of the changes or the record; but knows the impact the changes have had.

"I could beat Longbottom. Last time I rode against him was the Tour of the South West, which I think Darryl might have won. He was a good rider, but there were a few better than him, Darryl for one, possibly Paul Curran. I'm not putting him down, but I felt there were people better than him at the time. It's going to sound derogatory, but it's not sour grapes, more just a fact. These days time trialling has very little relevance to actual times. If you took these supervets turning in 33mph rides and put them against Tony Martin: would they win?

"With the aerodynamics, it's a different era, a different sort of sport now, and that's great, good, but, in comparison with the 1950s, the fixed wheels, the misty mornings, the herds of cows, the whole 50s package, it's not even remotely the same. I would limit it to the 1950s - until John Woodburn won the first '25' on gears; that was the period I would prefer. In between 1940 and 1960 the only thing that changed was John Woodburn rode gears, which they could well have done all that time ago if only they'd worked it out. There was a big chunk of time where the bicycle was how people got about. You rode a bike, you wore a flat cap and you lived on a council estate. Now the bicycle is more of a fetish object.

"It is marginal gains, and if I were up there now I would need to have it. But it's the position that has bought the big advance: the understanding of airflow. The gradual accretion has accelerated. But the money makes it a different thing altogether. You've got to put it in a wind tunnel; we could never have dreamed of, or even imagined, that. Where I grew up, and where I came from, it was so very different. Up at four or five o' clock in the morning, the tinkle of shoe plates on the road, the smell of embrocation, 5-4-3-2-1-GO! That is the essence of time trialling. The stillness of the morning, just you and the timekeeper, some banter. That was how I experienced time trialling and how I want to remember it. If I had gone on to do what I wanted to do I would have won the Tour de France, but that's how the dice were rolled. I regret it absolutely that I couldn't do it. I was married at 19 with children. I missed it, but I can't do anything about it."

It's not hard to notice the irony though; technological supremacist Alf Engers rails against technological supremacy in cycling. He's not railing I guess, just indicating that the sport has changed so much as to not really be comparable. He knows if he were riding now he'd be ahead of the curve, head to toe in the latest dimpled yaw deflectors, little jaggedy things that provoke boundary layers of air into misbehaving, body and bike shaped like a rocket. However, the answer remains the same: that's time trialling, and that's change over time. Alf still follows the sport, but his heroes, unsurprisingly, were his peers: "I admired Tommy Simpson. Beryl was head and shoulders above everybody else. She worked, she was the business. She used to work on Nim Carline's rhubarb farm. I admired her. Ray Booty; he was a trailblazer: he did it all, and he was still working."

And it comes back to work, to those who had to make sacrifices, to pursue the amateur lifestyle and try and reconcile the tension with an uneasy equilibrium between work, family, and sporting achievement. It's this that Alf admires, and regrets. The admiration for Beryl Burton is apposite: between them they are arguably the greatest exponents of the sport, possessed of a unique fanaticism and determination, a refusal to be beaten by anyone, whether that is other competitors, the authorities or members of their own family. Their careers spanned a period of enormous social and cultural change and they somehow rode blithely across and through these periods, as though ungoverned by the precise temporality that affects the rest of us, existing within a different sense of time where raw willpower and a solipsistic charisma transcends everything else. And like Alf, she worked hard.

"I had to work to survive and everything else took a back seat. As a baker, you make something, you sell it; there's an end product, that's it. When all these banks talk about a product, what product? What? You know what? Business? You're just moving figures around on paper. People seem to benefit from dishonesty. My mother used to say, 'honesty is the best policy'; is it buggery. I'd love to think so, but it isn't."

Things are either honest or dishonest, but for Alf it extends to an emotional as well as financial honesty. "The things I learned to do are no longer relevant in today's world. I can make sugar baskets and chocolates. You can't earn a living doing that. I went right back to the start, basic stuff. There was certainly no satisfaction, but I could earn a living. So I don't think, unless something happens, that I'm ever going to be satisfied with my lot. I couldn't have helped any kids training, because I was always working, full stop. And the job which I trained to do was useless in later life. The time trial was second best, the closest I could get to doing what I wanted to do, but work stopped it being anything more than that. I wasn't able to pass anything on, help any youngsters, because I was working. That is my big regret; that I wasn't able to pass anything that I've learned on to people. The only way we got a house was me doing two jobs permanently for a few years. At one point there was a bread strike, and I was getting two hours sleep a night – working two bakeries – a night shift and then the day shift. I had a permanent job and did agency work all over London. I'd go in and do the job, do a night job. Others were jobbing and it was like they had nowhere to live. They'd go and sleep on the Circle Line, come back and do another job. I've even done three separate bakeries in a day."

He regrets not being able to do for others what Alan Shorter did for him: to recognise potential, to guide, mentor and shape, to support and share in success. In conversation with Alf I find I am framing things within the prism of my lived experience. It's how I make sense of people, how I mediate their stories so I can write about them. And I'm aware that like Alf, I struggled to find fulfilment, or work out exactly who I was. I came to the conclusion that I was never going to find this mythical end goal, some place or time where everything suddenly dropped into place, so I stopped looking. I made similar, necessary compromises: I opted for the stability of a teaching job, rather than the endless uncertainty of writing. I found contentment in the fact that I couldn't find contentment. Work is a means to an end, it is my job, but at the same time I prefer to write, I prefer to ride my bike, I prefer to talk to people about their lives. In purely professional terms, there is a connection between Alf and my mum. Alf is a baker, my mum is a potter; they're similar professions, they have a product, they make things.

They are also deceptively simple things, flow activities. My mum is sometimes happy, then not happy because she's worrying about things: what people think, how much time we have left, the march of time, the lack of time, the void that stretches out before us and is both punctuated and punctured by the death of friends. A few years ago I recalibrated what I expected from life, away from some lofty pretension of success. It wasn't that I lowered my expectations; I just recalibrated the scale I used. For instance, most of my friends are bike riders. Very few bike riders ever win bike races, ever. Barely any of my friends have ever won anything, and many of them are much quicker than me. I once did a rough calculation when I broke the fifty minute barrier (35 years later than Alf on a bike made of purest speed and on a course with a two mile descent where I broke the 55mph barrier as well) that I was the 133rd fastest 25 miler in history. This is ranked against everyone ever, regardless of technology or equipment. For example, it's much faster than the Higginson twins and other people in the 1950s on very slow bikes, which really doesn't count unless, like me, you want it to. This was comforting. Nevertheless, I would have struggled to have finished in the top 133 in the National Championship in 1978.

It stands to reason that basing success on winning is going to end in failure. And yet our wider sense of fulfilment, the lessons we learn, seem predicated on a quest for bigger and better things, on absolute measures of success and headline events. All of this neglects the fact that if the big things are the definitive measure of success then we will only ever experience crushing disappointment and end up railing against the capricious Gods, the external forces destroying our dreams of immortality. I have a close friend, fellow writer and film-maker Steve Green . Our eyes met across a crowded train from Newport to Bristol because he had a copy of a magazine with pictures of Tommy Simpson in it and I had a track bike. A few years later, and Steve was best man at my wedding.

The week of the wedding, on the Tuesday before the Saturday, Steve's dad died. His dad was a carpenter, and had been working on a house. He had a heart attack in his van at lunch time and he was rushed to hospital. In amongst the overwhelming shock, grief and pain, Steve had to go and get the van.

The woman whose house it was came out to see him and asked him to come in for a minute. She spoke quietly as she showed him around: "It's hard to know what to say. I wanted you to know that it may not seem like much, but it is. Your Dad did work on and off for fifteen years in this house. He shaped it and renovated and restored it." She showed him the newel post and banister, the tongue and groove in the wall, the joists and joints, door frames and jambs. "He put in this beam... he redid the joists beneath the floor which we walk on every day..." And in that moment, as Steve retold the story on the morning of my wedding, a lot of things suddenly made more sense to me, because of the dedicated way his father did things. His craft and skill brought increments of joy to other people's lives, in a measurable way, and I think that it's hard to say it without sounding trite, but it seems to me important. All through his life (he was a cyclist, rode for the Clarion, and was a huge fan of the Milk Race) he worked in people's houses, fixing, repairing, building and mending. Everyday someone leans on or walks on something he made.

In Alf's living room there is an oak panelled bar, beams, dark wooden panels neatly interlocking which bring warmth, solidity and sense to the room; they bring comfort when the evening draws in, soften the atmosphere. Someone crafted them, aligned them carefully.

They bring happiness and comfort. And I'm reminded, in the writing of this book, of the Raymond Carver story 'A Small Good Thing', not only because the protagonist is a baker and Alf is a baker, but because of the underlying narrative and layers of meaning, of what it means to live and to be happy or not be happy.[42]

And I want to tell Alf, just like I want to tell my mum, that life is in the small details, the tiniest discernible ripples on the glassy surface of the lake, it's not the splash. Contentment is there, in the bigger things, but for most of us it's in the minutiae, it's even in the table I lean on whilst typing these words. Contentment is there, and we are ordinary people, and in our ordinary actions we provide and receive contentment. For Alf Engers, the ordinary and quotidian mingles with some extraordinary moments, which reach out to touch the lives of others and inspire them, to make them write books in response to an initial unexpected question across a crowded room of cyclists. But it's never that simple with Alf. "I don't think contentment is the word. I'm always searching. I'd like to achieve something. Don't ask me what it is, but I haven't found it yet. I don't feel like I've achieved anything yet, not at all. But what I can say? I haven't got any friends, neither has Jude, we've just got each other."

Judith speaks. She is always deliberate, thoughtful and prescient. I like her pronouncements. "You're too busy living your life; too busy getting old and you don't notice the changes around you."

Alf nods in silent acquiescence, then speaks. "We were all going to change the world in the 1960s and it didn't happen. I suppose it never will. The way people measure success for the most part is by material possessions. It's everywhere; my kids are like that. That's the way it is. Maybe one day I'll find it. I mean, I would like to be good at something. You hear about so and so being an expert on whales, how a whale swum up the Thames and suddenly you need an expert to say why it's swum up the Thames and is going round and round. I'd like to be an expert. Maybe I'm an expert on life.

Whatever it is, I'm still searching for it."

References

The Pedal Club
1. *The Unwomanly Face of War*, Svetlana Alexievich (2017)
2. "Aubade", *Collected Poems*, Philip Larkin (2003)

Lesson 1
3. *Family Britain 1951-57*, David Kynaston (2010)

Lesson 2
4. Len Finch http://www.bbc.co.uk/news/magazine-31013387
                                (accessed 14 May 2018)
5. http://www.britishpathe.com/video/cycle-speedway-1
                                (accessed 14 May 2018)
6. http://www.bbc.co.uk/news/magazine-31013387 (accessed 8 May 2017)

Lesson 3
7. "First Four Minute Mile"; https://www.youtube.comwatch?v=wTXoTn_5sI
                                (accessed 17 March 2018)

Lesson 5
8. Open Roads, David Saunders (http://northwoodwheelers.org.uk/index.
        php/open-roads/1951/55-june-1951 (accessed 19 April 2018)
9. "15 Vital Seconds in this Man's Life", *Cycling*, 3 June 1959
10. *ibid.*
11. *The Bicycle, UK*, 11 July 1951, p. 3
12. "Alf's Men Beat Olympic TT Teams!", *Cycling*, 30 May 1960

Lesson 7
13. "What kind of music are they playing?", *Roots, Radicals and Rockers*,
                Billy Bragg (2017)
14. *Free Cinema: a Manifesto, Karel Reisz*, T. Richardson and L. Anderson;
                                (1956)

Lesson 8
15. "High Priest Alf Crashes Back", Cycling, 9 March 1968
16. "Erring Alf?", *Cycling*, 16 March 1968
17. "Unfair to Alf", *Cycling*, 16 April 1968
18. "Engers: Serious soul behind a flippant mask", *Cycling*, 17 May 1969.
19. "Another Gem from Alf", *Cycling*, 18 May 1968

20. "Alf Strikes in the South", *Cycling*, 14 September 1968
21. "Birthday Cake for the Patissier", *Cycling*, 7 June 1969
22. RTTC Rules and Regulations:

21. Paced & Company Riding

Competitors must ride entirely alone and unassisted and not ride in company or take shelter   (commonly known as drafting) from other riders or vehicles. A competitor overtaking another must pass without receiving or giving shelter. The onus of avoiding company riding shall be upon the rider overtaken.

22. Use of Motor Vehicles

(a) A competitor shall not be preceded, accompanied, followed by or in any way receive assistance from a motorised vehicle or its occupants, except in events at distances of 100km or more to assist with a competitor's reasonable feeding and other requirements.

(b) In International selection events the Board may authorise motorised vehicles for the observance of a competitor(s).

(c) Where vehicles are to be authorised a full description of the vehicle and registration number shall be given to the event promoter prior to the start of the competitor. A competitor shall not be overtaken by his support vehicle more frequently than once every 10 miles. Where possible the vehicle must be driven at normal traffic speed and must not follow the competitor, nor impede or annoy other competitors. Any competitor whose authorised vehicle impedes or causes annoyance to any other competitor shall be liable to disqualification from the event. Where any other vehicle precedes or follows for any length of time, or frequently passes a competitor, that vehicle shall be deemed to be associated with that competitor who shall be liable to disqualification from the event.

Lesson 9
23. *Cycling*, 7 Jan 1970

Lesson 10
24. http://www.cyclingweekly.com/news/racing/british-racing/greatest-time-triallist-never-derek-cottingtons-disallowed-25-mile-record-1971-332192
(accessed 18 July 2017)
25. *ibid.*
26. "Pete Wells Wins", *Cycling*, 27 May 1972
27. "Engers shatters title field", *Cycling*, 10 June 1972

Lesson 11
28. "I'm glad it's all over", *Cycling*, 8 June 1974
29. "The Engers Method", *Cycling*, 19 October 1974
30. "Alf Astounds with Fifth and Best Title", *Cycling*, 7 June 1975
31. *ibid.*

Lesson 12

32. https://www.youtube.com/watch?v=q77GMkXzOVE!
                                    (accessed 12 March 2018)
33. "Engers the Giant", *Cycling*, 12 June 1976
34. *ibid.*
35. *ibid.*
36. "Engers Ban Now Cut to One Year", *Cycling*, 20 November, 1976
37. "Engers: serious soul behind a flippant mask", *Cycling*, 17 May, 1969

Lesson 13

38. "The Speed Machine", *Cycling*, 13 May 1978
39. *ibid.*
40. Editorial, *Cycling*, 28 October 1978

Lesson 14

41. *Alf Engers aka "The King"*, film by Ray Pascoe (Ray Films, 2014)
42. "A Small Good Thing", *Cathedral*, Raymond Carver (2009)

Bibliography

Bragg, Billy, 2017, *Roots, Radicals and Rockers: How Skiffle Changed the World*, London; Faber and Faber.

Burton, Beryl., 2008, *Personal Best*, Huddersfield; Springfield Books.

Hilton, Tim., 2011, *One More Kilometre and We're in the Showers*, London; Harper Perennial.

Kynaston, D., 2010, *Family Britain, 1951-1957; Tales of a New Jerusalem*, London; Bloomsbury

Pascoe, R., 2014, *Alf Engers AKA "The King"*, London, Ray Films

Thompson, B., 1988, *Alpaca to Skinsuit*, Ashford; Geerings of Ashford.

Whitfield, P., 2007, *12 Champions,* Charlbrook, Wychwood Publishing.

Whitfield, P., 2013, *Time, Speed and Truth: A History of Time-Trialling 1890–2010*

Williams, K., 2006, *John Woodburn: Fifty Years at the Top,* Charlbrook, Wychwood Publishing.

Also by Paul Jones

A Corinthian Endeavour:
the story of the National Hill Climb Championship.
pub. Mousehold Press, 2015.

"The text is littered with lines that cause you to pause: 'The clock ticks audibly on the wall within the silence of reminiscence, the seconds so palpably less precious now, in conversation, than they ever were in the race.' Jones is capable of astounding the reader."
Feargal Mckay; *Podium Café*

"Very well written and researched. I thoroughly enjoyed it."
Graham Snowdon; *Cycling Weekly, Daily Telegraph*

"A brilliant read."
Chris Sidwells

"He's taken a challenging subject and set the standard for all to try and beat. Anyone who tries is going to have to suffer horribly in the process. Jones's name is on the trophy, and his record will stand for years to come."
Scarlett Parker; author, *The Srampagnolo Tales*

"It takes considerable narrative skill to create a compulsive read out of eighteen chapters concerning a few minutes of ascendancy and Jones has this ability in spades ... an unexpected delight."
Brian Palmer; *www.thewashingmachinepost.net*

"A superb read and a must for anyone who loves bike racing and the history of the sport."
Larry Hickmott, *Velo UK*

"The book does not merely catalogue the events but gives background material, personally researched, to let the reader understand what makes these 'stick men' tick.."
Peter Underwood, *Veteran Cycle Club*